The Homebrewed Christianity
Guide to Jesus

The Homebrewed Christianity Guide to Jesus

Lord, Liar, Lunatic . . . Or Awesome?

TRIPP FULLER
AUTHOR AND SERIES EDITOR

Fortress Press
Minneapolis

THE HOMEBREWED CHRISTIANITY GUIDE TO
JESUS
Lord, Liar, Lunatic . . . Or Awesome?

Cover design: Jesse Turri
Book design: PerfecType, Nashville, TN

Library of Congress Cataloging-in-Publication Data is available
Paperback ISBN: 978-1-4514-9957-5
eBook ISBN: 978-1-5064-0125-6

The paper used in this publication meets the minimum
requirements of American National Standard for Information Sciences—Permanence of Paper for Printed Library
Materials, ANSI Z329.48-1984.

Manufactured in the U.S.A.

Contents

Homebrewed Christianity Guide: Series Preface vii

The Homebrewed Posse xi

Lord, Liar, Lunatic . . . or Just *Freaking* Awesome 1

Jesus' Jewish Neighborhood 23

Abba Says, "Drop the G" 41

Reading the Gospels Heresy-Free 65

Anselm, Luther, and the Cootie Collector 89

Getting High with Jesus 111

Turning Jesus Down 133

The Skeptic and the Believer 155

Acknowledgments 177

Notes 179

Series Introduction

You are about to read a guidebook. Not only is the book the sweet "guide book" size, shaped perfectly to take a ride in your back pocket, but the book itself was crafted with care by a real-deal theology nerd. Here's the thing. The Homebrewed Christianity Guide series has one real goal: we want to think *with* you, not *for* you.

The whole "homebrew" metaphor grows from my passion for helping anyone who wants to geek out about theology to do so with the best ingredients around. That's why I started the Homebrewed Christianity podcast in 2008, and that's why I am thrilled to partner with Fortress Press's Theology for the People team to produce this series. I am confident that the church has plenty of intelligent and passionate people who want a more robust conversation about their faith.

A podcast, in case you're wondering, is like talk radio on demand without the commercials. You download a file and listen when, if, where, and how long you want. I love the podcast medium. Short of talking one-on-one, there's hardly a more intimate presence than speaking to someone in their earbuds as they're stuck in traffic, on the treadmill, or washing dishes. When I started the podcast,

I wanted to give anyone the option of listening to some of the best thinkers from the church and the academy.

Originally, the podcast was for friends, family, and my local pub theology group. I figured people in the group were more likely to listen to a podcast than read a giant book. So as the resident theology nerd, I read the books and then interviewed the authors. Soon, thousands of people were listening. Since then the audience has grown to over fifty thousand unique listeners each month and over a million downloads. A community of listeners, whom we call Deacons, grew, and we've got a cast of co-hosts and regular guests.

Over the better part of a decade, I have talked to scores of theologians and engaged with the Deacons about these conversations. It has been a real joy. Every time I hear from a listener, I do the happy dance in my soul.

And here's the deal: I love theology, but I love the church more. I am convinced that the church can really make a difference in the world. But in order to do that, it needs to face reality rather than run from it. The church must use its brain, live its faith, and join God in working for the salvation of the world. And that's what these books are all about.

We often open and close the podcast by reminding listeners that we are providing the ingredients so that they can brew their own faith. That's the same with these books. Each author is an expert theological brewer, and they've been asked to write from their own point of view. These guidebooks are not boringly neutral; instead, they are zestily provocative, meant to get you thinking and brewing.

I look forward to hearing from you on the Speakpipe at HomebrewedChristianity.com and meeting you at an HBC 3D event. We can drink a pint and talk about this book, how you agree and disagree with it. Because if we're talking about theology, the world is a better place.

And remember: Share the Brew!

Tripp Fuller

The Homebrewed Posse

Whether it's the podcast, the blog, or live events, Homebrewed Christianity has always been a conversation, and these books are no different. So inside of this and every volume in the HBC book, you'll be hearing from four members of the Homebrewed community. They are:

THE BISHOP

The Bishop: Kindly, pastoral, encouraging. She's been around the block a few times, and nothing ruffles her feathers. She wants everyone to succeed, and she's an optimist, so she knows they will.

THE ELDER

The Elder: Scolding, arrogant, know-it-all. He's old and disgruntled, the father figure you can never please. He loves quoting doctrine; he's the kind of guy who controls every church meeting because he knows Roberts Rules of Order better than anyone else.

THE DEACON

The Deacon: Earnest, excited, energetic. He's a guy who has just discovered HBC, and he can't get enough of it. He's a cheerleader, a shouter, an encourager. He's still in his first naïveté.

THE ACOLYTE

The Acolyte: Smart, inquisitive, skeptical. She's the smartest student in your confirmation class. She's bound to be a biologist or a physicist, and she's skeptical of all the hocus pocus of Christianity. But she hasn't given up on it yet, so her questions come from the heart. She really wants to know if all this stuff works.

We look forward to continuing the conversation with you, online and in-person!

Lord, Liar, Lunatic . . .
or Just *Freaking* Awesome

I have discovered a secret way of solving the most per-
plexing theological questions. My college roommate
and I invented it in our dorm room as a way of finding
answers to some of our most contentious debates. We
were religion and philosophy majors, which means we
argued about religion and politics as a kind of recreational
sport. When we arrived at an intractable difference of
opinions, we settled it like any nineteen-year-old scholar
should—by playing a video game. We settled our disputes
over a game of Madden 2001, to be exact. We decided that
the best way for the Holy Spirit to lead us to a solution to
our dilemma was through a simulated NFL game. It's the
postmodern version of casting lots! Will God save every
human who has ever lived? Yes. Is there anything more
annoying than a libertarian Calvinist with a goatee? No.

Would Jesus invade Iraq? No. Was Stryper or Guns N' Roses the greatest hair-metal band? GNR, but I am still protesting that decision.

Perhaps the most memorable game settled a question about Jesus you never even thought to ask: *Did Jesus have nocturnal emissions?* The answer was yes.

The full humanity of Jesus is something every Christian affirms, but when it comes to discussing his journey through adolescence, we like to keep it vague—"He grew in wisdom and in stature" is the only mention in the Bible of his teen years. Of course, we don't spend much time thinking about Jesus having lice in his hair or pooping, even if he did such things in the holiest of ways. Somehow this real-deal human being has been redacted from our theology. What's left is less a story about a homeless first-century Jew and prophet of God's kingdom than a theological conclusion: Jesus is God.

Even worse, many Christians believe this conclusion is patently obvious. They assume that Jesus overtly claimed that he was God, that it's recorded all through the Bible, and that if you don't affirm this truth, you may be in eternal jeopardy. This precarious conclusion is often put forward in the form of a trilemma popularized by C. S. Lewis: Jesus claimed to be the Lord, so Jesus is either the Lord, or else he's a liar or a lunatic. Giving the hearer two answers that lead to damnation is not exactly opening up the dilemma.

As a pretty big fan of Jesus, let me just say that the trilemma is ridiculous. I call Jesus my Lord and Savior, but the demand that each of us respond to Jesus in such a reductive way is dumbfounding. In fact, it only takes five minutes with a biblical scholar to realize how preposterous the idea is. The historical Jesus didn't claim to be God, biblical scholars will tell you, but his followers saw him as divine when God raised him from the dead. (For this reason, some add "legend" as a fourth alliterative option in the trilemma, proposing that Jesus' followers exaggerated it.) What exactly that event means for us today is an open question with a bunch of plausible answers. As you read this book I hope you will not only think through the questions you bring and the answers you muster, but also come to appreciate those of others who follow Jesus.

Just the idea of writing a "guide to Jesus" is presumptuous. I'm pretty sure that two billion Christians are not sitting around waiting for some dude with a podcast to

---

If a twenty-first-century discussion of Jesus starts out with wet dreams, then I'll stick with Science Digest.

THE ACOLYTE

---

finally guide them to an image of Jesus worth their allegiance. Nor is writing such a guide easy. If a guide to the economy, the ecosystem, your own family, or even the Lego version of the Millennium Falcon is complex, why should Jesus be simple? (Hint: he isn't.)

I hope this book gets you beyond the limits of Lewis's saying and lets you see Jesus as just freaking awesome. ("Lord, Liar, Lunatic . . . or Freaking Awesome" was supposed to be the subtitle of this book, but the publisher dropped "Freaking." While I understand the decision, I want to say something about that. "Freaking" is a title that confers on Jesus an *overwhelming level of awesomeness*. Not "awesome" as applied to a good movie, the perfect date, or a Counting Crows concert. *Freaking awesome* is ontologically distinct and prior to anything that is simply awesome. To say that Jesus is *freaking awesome* is to say that the person of Jesus participates in the awe-someness that initiates and sustains all of creation. Likewise, when we encounter this awesomeness in Jesus, it can freak us out because realizing that we are completely known is freaky, and to receive this identity as God's beloved through a homeless first-century Jew is *just freaking awesome*.)

THE ELDER

How can Jesus be homeless when he's taken up residence in my heart?

Christology Is Crazy

When Christians try to answer the question "Who is Jesus?" they are engaging in what theologians call *Christology*. True, it's not nearly as cool a name as the doctrine of the Holy Spirit, *pneumatology*, or the End Times, *eschatology*, but what Christology lacks in a sweet-sounding label, it makes up for in sheer bravado. Christology is just plain crazy. It is ridiculous. Most any spiritual person could have a conversation about the Spirit, and half of the

movies coming out of Hollywood are about some dysto-
pian apocalyptic future, but when Christians start talking
Christology, people get nervous. That's because Jesus was
a homeless, itinerant, first-century rabbi who talked about
the end of the world, taught in parables even his disciples
couldn't follow, and ended up dying on a Roman cross as a
failed political resistor. *That* is the Jesus we call the Christ,
the Son of the living God, the First Born of all creation, the
Image of the invisible God, the eternal Logos, and all of the
other christological titles packed into the New Testament.

While the titles easily roll off our tongues in worship
and are around every corner in the Bible, how to apply
them is not immediately obvious. Personally, I love them,
sing them, and proclaim them, but I think we would be
doing ourselves and Jesus' PR firm a favor if the church
were a little more aware of how we sound to outsiders. For
many who grew up in the church, even those who no longer attend regularly, identifying Jesus as the Son of God
is completely reasonable. We may roll our eyes whenever
the latest New Atheist prophet or biblical scholar gets on
TV mouthing off all sorts of reasons to doubt these names
and claims, but when Tom Cruise explains the veracity of
L. Ron Hubbard's science fiction we roll them for a different reason. It's absurd.

Yes, that was a Scientology joke. But if you simply
switch their religious myth with ours, you get the point.
Christology is packed full of strong, absurd, and tenuous
affirmations about Jesus. What we say about Jesus and
even how we celebrate God's work in him is shocking
when looked at from the outside, and it always has been.

Pliny the Younger is not simply the name of Russian
River's legendary Triple IPA, available for two wonderful

weeks in February. Pliny was also the governor of Pontus, province of Asia Minor, from 111 to 113 CE. One of the few times Jesus and the early church is mentioned by someone not part of a Christian community is in the correspondence between Pliny and the Roman emperor Trajan. Below is a wonderfully revealing piece describing how the first Christians sounded to outsiders. For context, Pliny is checking in with Trajan about his legal process for people brought before him on charges of being Christian. This means that they likely refused to worship the Roman gods, which was a serious political offense.

> They asserted, however, that the sum and substance of their fault or error had been that they were accustomed to meet on a fixed day before dawn and sing responsively a hymn to Christ as to a god, and to bind themselves by oath, not to some crime, but not to commit fraud, theft, or adultery, not falsify their trust, nor to refuse to return a trust when called upon to do so. When this was over, it was their custom to depart and to assemble again to partake of food—but ordinary and innocent food. Even this, they affirmed, they had ceased to do after my edict by which, in accordance with your instructions, I had forbidden political associations. Accordingly, I judged it all the more necessary to find out what the truth was by torturing two female slaves who were called deaconesses. But I discovered nothing else but depraved, excessive superstition.[1]

Pliny nails it. These Christians are straight-up weird, singing songs to the cross-dead Jesus as if to a god, sharing normal meals of bread and wine, promising to be ethically rigorous and trustworthy, and even ordaining female slaves as deaconesses! The only thing immediately obvious

---

A beautiful display of historic Christianity! Sounds just like my diocese (except for the slave part).

THE BISHOP

---

to Pliny about these Christians was that their central affirmations and practices are odd. He doesn't want to destroy the Christians, he just wants them to keep it weird on the down-low and avoid messing with Caesar's kingdom.

Today things have changed. The empire that Pliny represented eventually merged with the cross-bearer's fan club, and the reign of Christendom meant that the church's affirmations of Jesus became culturally normative. The affirmations that "Jesus is the Christ" and "Jesus is Lord" became unavoidable in the West, and this has been the case for so long that most of us Christians are just now coming to terms with how weird we sound when we talk about Jesus. It can be embarrassing. Of course, we could just stay in our Christian circles or dodge the topic when in mixed company, but if we treat the question of Jesus' identity with the seriousness his disciples always have, it's hard to imagine we can really leave it unexamined.

Therefore, I want to suggest a theological rule: *Keep it weird.*

If your Christology isn't weird, you're doing it wrong. The church's theological confessions about Christ are not suddenly embarrassing; they always have been. Join the parade! It's not like it takes a pluralistic culture informed by science to realize that identifying a dead homeless Jew as the Son of the living God is absurd. It is. Let's own it. But instead of just regurgitating it without reflection and throwing it at our befuddled neighbors as a trilemma with eternal consequences, let's let the weirdness seep into our own imaginations.

Keeping Christology Weird

"Without risk, no faith. Faith is the contradiction between the infinite passion of inwardness and the objective uncertainty. If I comprehend God objectively, I do not have faith; but because I cannot do this, I must have faith."[2] Søren Kierkegaard said that. He was a nineteenth-century Danish philosopher obsessed with the absurdity of the incarnation—that is, the doctrine of Jesus' birth.

Søren had significant doubts himself, so he explored the paradox of the God-man. In his day there was a debate between a theologian named Jacobi and a doubting philosopher named Lessing. Lessing insisted that he wanted to believe in Christ, but because of his doubts, he could not muster the courage to make the jump. For Lessing, the problem with the claim that Jesus was God was that those trying to prove it could only point to historical proof. He thought that pointing only to texts—whether sacred or historical—could not settle a question this big. To demonstrate the presence of the eternal in a particular historical event was something Lessing couldn't manage, but that didn't stop Jacobi from trying!

Kierkegaard's response to their debate was surprising in that he chided Jacobi and not Lessing. In Lessing, Kierkegaard saw someone who was actually taking the

---

I used to think there was evidence that demanded a verdict, too. Then I decided to use my brain.

THE ELDER

---

christological claim with utter seriousness. Lessing recognized that faith requires—indeed, demands—a decision, a leap. Historically, there can be no security in affirming that God was indeed *in* Christ. The results are always going to be approximate and could never justify an infinite concern. Basically, Kierkegaard was saying that even if historians could make demonstrable claims about who Jesus was, that wouldn't create the conditions for genuine faith. Since the case can't be persuasive, Christ's authoritative call to faith is offensive.

For Kierkegaard, faith is not merely explaining the idea that Jesus is God so that it becomes reasonable or palatable; faith is facing the possibility of the offense and choosing to believe rather than be offended. As Kierkegaard loved to point out, it was Jesus himself who said, "Blessed are those who are not offended by me." This act of faith is the decision of the individual alone—no professor, preacher, or Sunday School teacher can make it for you.

Kierkegaard said that despite God's best efforts, there were some amazing Christian theologians who had managed to make believing way too easy. He was being sarcastic. So easy did they make the faith that there was no need for real faith. In turning the leap of faith into an easy act of intellectual assent, these theologians actually undid the conditions necessary for the possibility of faith. They turned faith from an encounter with *someone* to an idea about *something*. But Kierkegaard objected, saying that faith by its nature needed to be directed at a *subject*, not an *object*.

I'm with ol' Søren on this. Christian faith is not about learning how to crack God's true/false test, but about coming to know yourself before God. In order to preserve faith, Kierkegaard set out to make belief more difficult. In doing so, he was actually making genuine faith possible. For Søren, Christianity was not a doctrine, but a decision. And truth was not a set of propositions, but a mode of being in the world.

For me, Kierkegaard haunts all my attempts to rationalize and wrestle with God, and especially with God's presence in Christ. On my most confident days, when my convictions seem to be well constructed and viable, good ol' Søren is giggling in the corner at the entire intellectual exercise.[3] It's crucial for contemporary Christians to grapple with Kierkegaard's logic here because only when we become acquainted with the absurdity of christological claims can we truly affirm our faith.

In his book *Philosophical Investigations*, Kierkegaard wrote that there were really two different types of teachers. One is like Socrates, the great Greek philosopher, and the other is like Jesus. Socrates saw that truth was present in his students, but they needed the coaxing and prodding of a skilled teacher's questions to send them on the path to discover it more fully. My old geometry teacher, Mr. Robinson, was an excellent teacher, but he himself was not necessary for the truth I discovered in his class. There are plenty of awesome geometry teachers who have been the occasion for their students' learning, but what is gained is always the *teaching* and not the *teacher*. Once you get the theorem, you can know its truth in the same way that the teacher does.

To understand Socrates is to realize you owe him nothing, but to know Jesus as the Christ is to owe him everything. For Kierkegaard, the major contrast between the two is this: for the follower of Jesus, the occasion, condition, and content of faith is inextricably connected to the teacher himself. In fact, the object of faith is not the teaching at all but the teacher—the one in whom the infinite God was present. You do not come to know the truth; you

---

I don't know what that means, but I hope to be known by what that means. Fancy.

THE DEACON

---

come to be known by the truth. As long as the Christian is defined as one for whom God was in Christ, what you gain through faith doesn't make you indistinguishable from Christ. Instead, you become known by Christ—the very teacher himself.

In the end, Kierkegaard is right to suggest that the craziness of the claim might mean a true disciple is properly labeled a lunatic. The Christ event is not about its concrete historical *whatness* but the paradoxical *thatness* of the claim itself. It makes no difference if you were one of Jesus' original twelve disciples in the first century or one of the more than two billion in the twenty-first, for the incarnation can't be seen or comprehended. Time and location are eclipsed, and faith demands a leap! I don't think Søren is lying about the built-in lunacy in the confession of Jesus' lordship; it's just that the only clear thing about the paradox of the incarnation is that it's absurd—and freaking awesome.

We Aren't in Denmark Anymore

Kierkegaard lived in a world where Jacobi and Lessing battled it out in the public square, a time when the church had a privileged place in society and the few skeptics could joust with the most gifted apologists for the enjoyment of the cultured elite. Nearly everyone considered himself or herself a believer, and it took some intense provocation to crack through the armor that Christendom had draped over the hearts of its devotees. Today, the skeptic and the believer are not public debate partners as much as they are two different voices within each of us. Some of us have had one voice affirmed and the other shouted down, but they are within us nonetheless.

Over the past seven years, I've had the privilege talking to hundreds of amazing theologians, authors, and scholars on my podcast, *Homebrewed Christianity*. We provide zesty audiological ingredients from all corners of the

Christian world for people to brew their own faith. I often get emails from conservative evangelical ministers or chat with them after live podcast events, and they tell me the show is a guilty pleasure for them, as the podcast is usually considered theologically progressive. And sometimes I hear from longtime atheists who listen in for laughs only to find more thoughtful theology than what they had originally rejected. Some have even shared with me religious experiences they've never been able to explain. It's always an honor to have people get real with me about their faith journeys (I'm also a pastor), but what's crazy is how many of us are living as both skeptics and believers. We need the freedom to embrace that. It's a wonderful place to live if we can let ourselves be there.

If the skeptic and the believer have moved in—and they're not leaving anytime soon—then we should take stock of what that means. It's popular to use the word *postmodern* to describe our situation these days. People have a variety of either positive or negative different feelings about postmodernity, but I think it's wise to at least acknowledge its arrival. So, let's describe this postmodern consciousness and five elements that shape it.[4]

Historical consciousness emerged at the end of modernity. We came to realize that our place in the world—our culture, family, religion, and more—is rather arbitrary. We're thrown into the world, and when we awaken to our own humanity, most of what is possible and available to us is already determined. For example, had I been born in Saudi Arabia, there is little chance I would be writing this book on Jesus. If you were born there, you probably wouldn't be reading this. More than just my own historicity, the entire planet's has become an object of reflection.

We know so much about human history that it's hard to say it's going somewhere, that it has a direction or goal (that's what theologians call *teleology*, if you want to impress your friends with a sweet *-ology* word).

Social consciousness is that haunting feeling that whatever we want to call knowledge is actually a social construction. We may hold certain truths to be self-evident, but when it comes to even basic concepts, like the equality of all people, Thomas Jefferson and Barack Obama had very different visions. In the very act of learning to use language, we end up adopting the world as it opens or closes to us. Underneath the world, we engage with institutional and systemic powers that operate upon us, our imaginations, and our physical selves. We know there is no generic human being, for we are a humanity awash in difference. And apart from our class, gender, race, and other socially structuring particularities, it is impossible to grasp any one of us.

Pluralist consciousness is pretty simple. You and I live in a world occupied by people of many different faiths and those with no faith. Most of us have neighbors and coworkers who practice other religions and are clearly not agents of Satan. We also have access to TV and the

THE DEACON

Seems funny now, but I just got over losing my youth ministry job for doing holy yoga. #Hindu #HIMdont

internet and recognize that each religion takes all kinds of different shapes across the globe. Each religion has awesome versions and ugly versions, peaceful versions and warring versions. But it is definitely not clear why there are so many religions if there is one God. Given that the dominant narrative of Christianity says that everyone everywhere must repent and accept Christ's work on their behalf, its lack of persuasiveness to our non-Christian neighbors raises some big questions.

Cosmic consciousness is a mind blower. You and I and Jesus are part of a history 13.8 billion years long. We are made up of really old stardust that was previously part of other carbon-based entities. The star our planet revolves around is one of over 200 billion stars; eventually our sun will eat our home, and earth will be no more. Even human life on this planet is not what it used to be. You and I (and Jesus?) are the products of natural selection and genetic mutation. To say that one person on this little planet is the image of the invisible God is far from obvious.

You are correct. This is an astronomical issue.

THE ACOLYTE

False consciousness is the recognition that there is no longer a harbor for purely rational, objective thought. It's hard to develop clear and persuasive lines of argument when you can no longer even trust yourself. Maybe you believe in an afterlife because you fear death or see God equally in all religions because you don't want to be rejected by your neighbors. In the past, debates over any particular truth, including God, used to be a battle over the conclusions. After the "masters of suspicion"— Marx, Nietzsche, and Freud—the people who started the argument themselves became subject to critique. Once suspicion is raised about the origin of a truth claim—in other words, the person who makes the claim—finality about a conclusion will never be reached. Philosopher Paul Ricoeur called this the beginning of a "postreligious period of faith." The battle line between the atheist and the theist is no longer clear and external; it's inside you and me.

From Jesus to the Christ

Today, there are a number of fundamental challenges to Christology. What was most obvious to Lessing is perhaps even more intense today—lately, it's called the "quest for the historical Jesus." Once you become aware that there is no single authoritative source for objective historical truth about Jesus, it's a bit hard to choose between him as liar, lunatic, or Lord. Some still deny that we can use the methods of historians to figure out who Jesus was; they continue to argue that we should base our decision on what Jesus said in the Gospels. That argument, how- ever, is becoming completely irrelevant in a world where historians question whether the Gospels themselves are historically accurate.

Not only does the New Testament itself have mul- tiple and conflicting views of what it means to call Jesus the Christ, but within the early church the perspectives continued to grow and expand. Of course, this includes a lot of people who were labeled "heretics," but the fact that the label was applied to the historical losers should give us pause before we ignore them. For example, taken alone Paul seems oblivious or disinterested to most of the sayings and deeds of Jesus, instead focusing exclusively on the cross and resurrection to communicate his own particular Christology.

Once you look under the christological hood, you find a doctrine that required ecclesiastical councils to polish, creeds and a hierarchy to enforce, and a never-ending

---

What a beautiful example of God's providential hand.

THE BISHOP

---

chain of theological texts to refine. In different cultures and in different times, the confession "Jesus is the Christ" has been explained differently. It has answered a whole bunch of different questions. For example, I don't know anyone who loses much sleep trying to figure out just how God was going to trick the devil and steal back the souls of us sinful people; however, there was a time that question mattered, and Jesus helped the church answer it.

We may not be concerned about Satan, but in light of contemporary science, it's reasonable to wonder if God really does *act* in any way in the world. So much of what we experience is now accounted for scientifically, whereas in the past spiritual phenomena were seen as a mysterious realm where angels played. And if we can't account for

God's activity in the world today, how can we claim that God was uniquely acting in Jesus? The Gospels themselves describe Jesus performing miracles, being conceived by a virgin, walking on water, bringing people back from the dead, and of course rising from the dead and ascending to the right hand of God the Father. So our primary documents about the life of Jesus make some pretty outrageous claims, at least in our scientific age.

These different challenges to historic Christology don't end the conversation, but they can't be ignored either. Many Christians are tempted to figure out a way to avoid these challenges altogether. Some look to the historic tradition of the church and say it's all or nothing—take it or leave it. Others defend a version of scriptural authority that insists that the Bible is completely different than any other text in the world and that to treat it properly requires unquestioned allegiance to its content.

Once I was talking to a famous evangelical theologian who had just published a very popular book of theology and was speaking at several different schools and seminaries about the text. I told him that I appreciated his inclusion of early church perspectives on theology, but I concluded that his book could have been written in the seventeenth century. He seemed to ignore all recent scholarship. In the introduction, he rather briefly explained why history, science, philosophy, religious pluralism, and such do not threaten the authority of the Bible, and then he proceeded to write a theology treatise that someone in the fourth century would love. He and I had a heated but respectful conversation, and it was clear that these problems had bothered him as he prepared to write, but in the book itself they didn't make it out of chapter one. You see, he had settled the postmodern challenges *before* he started writing, whereas I couldn't imagine a Christian theology that treated all intellectual challenges as opponents to be demolished prior to theologizing.

Today, when the skeptic and the believer both live within us, we must take the questions into the process of our theology. If we try to suppress our doubts, hide from the challenges, or ignore legitimate questions, we are not being awesome Christians but crappy apologists. Just think of that passage from 1 Peter: "In your hearts revere Christ as Lord. Always be ready to make your defense to anyone who demands from you an account-ing for the hope that is in you."[5] What we are defending is the hope! Hope, not an objective fact. There is a big difference between giving an account of the superiority of West Coast IPAs over those malt-bombs from the East

---

It's an official Homebrewed rule. If you are gonna call an IPA good, it's gotta be at least as nice as Sculpin.

THE DEACON

Coast and giving an account of your love for your partner. No one is going to hear me describe why I love my wife and tell me, "Oops, I just fell in love with her too after that thorough description." If I do a decent job describing the love I have for her, those listening are more likely to understand why I love her and be inspired by that love.

You cannot put love in a math equation, and you cannot turn hope into a syllogism.

This is good news for the skeptical believer, for as we live life in the way of Jesus, we can carry our questions with us, stay crazy, and keep figuring out how to speak about the one who puts hope on our horizon. Maybe a good way to capture this idea is to establish some new guidelines for the believing skeptic:

1. Keep Christology crazy.
2. When doing theology, all questions worth asking should be asked and then asked again.
3. At some point theology turns into doxology.[6] You won't know when.
4. If you are already practicing the way of Jesus, your theology will suck less.[7]

THE BISHOP

That's why we wear black robes, light candles, burn incense, and chant songs in Latin. Keeping it crazy with the liturgy.

As we continue our conversation about Jesus, I want to let you know a couple things. *I am a huge Jesus fan.* While I tend to hang out with pretty progressive Christians, my Christology is significantly higher than most of them.[8] This means I will probably make most readers uncomfortable at some point. My evangelical friends may get a bit squeamish about *how* I develop different ideas, and my progressive friends may not go along with *what* I end up saying. I bet my "Christian atheist" friends will think I'm crazy, too, but that's cool. After all, it is Christology!

Remember, Jesus is freaking awesome, and Christology is crazy!

Christology is the most diverse and divisive doctrine the church has. At the heart of the Christian faith is the claim that our relationship to God is uniquely mediated by Jesus Christ. As Christians we cannot describe who God is and what God is like without telling the story of this one person—Jesus of Nazareth. Since the early church, we have been trying to describe and share just how it is that the one true God of Israel was present in Jesus, and how God remains so. For those of us who believe that God was in Christ reconciling the world to Godself, then the question of who Jesus is cannot be the only question we ask. We must also ask, *who was that God in Christ?*

The reason we tell the story is not because Jesus had some good ideas, not even because he was a prophet, a proto-feminist-Marxist-hippie-anarchist, or even the most zesty human to rock planet earth. For those of us who call Jesus the Christ, we cannot talk about Jesus apart from talking about God's self-revelation in Jesus. Yes, Jesus was an actual historical person, but for me and many other Christians, it's not simply what he said and did that's awesome. It is what God accomplished and continues to do in and through Christ that is freaking awesome.

Enough with this crazy talk. Let's get crazy.

Jesus' Jewish Neighborhood

Jesus was Jewish. I know it seems obvious, but here's a crazy fact: until fairly recently, scholarship about Jesus didn't really take his Jewishness into account. Throughout the early church, the Middle Ages, and the Reformation, the experts who studied Jesus in the Bible pretty much ignored the fact that Jesus, his disciples, his opponents, and just about everyone who wrote about him in the New Testament were *Jews*. That means Augustine, Aquinas, Luther—they all overlooked the fact that Jesus and the whole cast of characters were Jewish. And to make it even crazier, some of them (cough, Luther, cough) were vociferously anti-Semitic. There are a whole bunch of ancient church sermons that refer to the Jews as "Christ-killers" while neglecting to inform the congregation that Jesus himself and many of the folks with "St." before their names were Jews, too.

THE ELDER

A non-Jewish Jesus is as reasonable as a History Channel special reporting that aliens helped build the pyramids.

It wasn't until the late nineteenth century, during the so-called quest for the historical Jesus, that theologians and Bible scholars began taking Jesus' Jewishness into account when they wrote about him. And nowadays, you couldn't get a paper about Jesus presented at the Society of Bible Literature—the major nerd gathering of Bible scholars—without a few paragraphs about Jesus' Jewishness to kick it off.

I've fallen into this error myself. For example, in the Gospels, Jesus talks about the "Son of Man" and the "Son of God." Before I ever read a historian, I assumed the former title referred to Jesus' humanity and the latter to his divinity. Little did I know that when a first-century Jew heard "Son of Man," it didn't mean what I thought it meant. "Son of Man" was the most lofty title available for Jesus to give himself, while "Son of God" could be applied to almost any good Jewish figure.[1] I had applied the church's fifth-century Christology to the first-century Gospels.

Jesus' Jewishness is important for many reasons, but perhaps the biggest is simply this: he was born, lived, and died within the period known as Second Temple Judaism (the first temple was the one built by Solomon in 957 BCE and destroyed by the Egyptian Pharaoh a few

decades later; the second temple was built after the Israelites returned to Israel in the sixth century BCE, following their captivity in Babylon). What drove Jesus' own
mission, framed his identity, inspired his preaching, and
nursed his own spirituality was his Jewish faith. There is

Is it wrong for so many
Christians to think Jews
need to switch religions?

THE DEACON

no evidence that he intended to start a new religion, let
alone one destined to be made up almost entirely of non-
Jews (aka gentiles). To ignore these dynamics and project
back onto Jesus something different is a serious mistake.
Not only has the church managed to miss the very thing
Jesus was passionate about—what he called the "kingdom
of God"—but a Jesus deprived of his Jewish heritage has
led Christians toward a horrendous anti-Semitism, the
church's most glaring perversion throughout history.

It's important to
recognize that just as
God will be faithful to
the covenant in Christ,

THE BISHOP

so too will God be faithful to the
covenant with Abraham and Sarah.

In Jesus' day, a Jew's identity was shaped by a number of historical factors, including the occupation of the land by Rome, the centering presence of the temple in Jerusalem, and the people's apocalyptic hope. ("Apocalyptic hope" is a sweet way scholars describe religious visions in which God dramatically intervenes to fix things. On paper it comes out sounding like science fiction.)

When Jesus came along, the people of Israel were not in exile. They were living in their homeland, but under Roman rule. Since God had promised to bless them, give them their Promised Land, and have them serve as a light to the nations, it was troubling to many Jews that they were a conquered people. Herod the Great and his three kids who took over after him—all of them Jewish governors doing Rome's bidding—were hated. They were seen as professional compromisers who served on Rome's behalf, keeping the vast majority of the people in poverty and under constant threat of violence.

There was no separation of church and state in the Roman Empire, Jerusalem included, and therefore poli-

---

THE ELDER

Did they have a state-funded theme park based on Noah's Ark?

---

tics were theological for the Jewish people. The Roman question dominated much of the theo-political fervor of the time, leading the people to ask a series of questions: When will God free us from this Roman oppression? When will God's anointed one, the Messiah, come to rule again over God's people? When will history demonstrate

that the good God of Israel is indeed the good God of all?
No matter the specific answers to these questions, nearly
all included the removal of Rome and its puppet leaders
from the throne.

First-Century Judaism(s)

The diversity within Second Temple Judaism is written
all over the Gospels. Jesus encountered the Pharisees,
Sadducees, Herodians, Zealots, and more. Each of these
theo-political parties had its own answer to the problem
of Roman rule, and each thought that its version of faithfulness would bring an end to that rule. The Sadducees
emphasized "your best life now." They were pragmatic,
compromising their faith and cooperating with Herod,
and they were the dominant religious leaders in Jerusalem.

The Sadducees rejected any belief in the afterlife.
That's why they tried to corner Jesus by asking him who
the husband of a woman who had successively married

That's why they
were so sad-you-see.
#VBSlessons

THE DEACON

---

three brothers should be.[2] They thought that if the Scriptures said to marry your dead brother's wife, then it would
get pretty creepy in heaven if she had been through all
the siblings. It seems a bit of an odd question, and more
than a bit passive aggressive. Why didn't they just say,
"What gives you the right to offer people eternal life,
something even God doesn't? Nowhere in the Torah is

there any mention of postmortem existence. If God didn't tell Moses, why would God tell you?!" That would have been a more pointed question, but the Sadducees probably didn't ask it because they already held the minority position on the afterlife—all the other factions believed in it.

The Zealots were Jewish revolutionaries who had a clear answer to Roman occupation: military resistance. Their confidence that God had promised the land and autonomous rule resulted in various forms of violence, both large-scale uprisings and small-scale terrorist attacks. They became a distinct movement prior to the first Jewish-Roman War (66–73 CE), but they were present in pockets and with different intensities throughout Israel. Popular Zealot leaders may have risen to prominence in different areas and for different reasons, but they all met the same fate: death at the hands of the Romans.

These are just two of the theo-political parties in Jerusalem at Jesus' time, and they were each fomenting revolution in one form or another. One way that Rome deterred political rebellion was through crucifixion. When Jesus was an adolescent, a Zealot uprising captured the Galilean city of Sepphoris. The Roman army promptly took it back and crucified two thousand revolutionaries, sending quite a message.[3] The Gospel of Luke identifies Simon the Zealot as one of Jesus' disciples, and the question of violence is clearly a live one among the disciples right up to the Garden of Gethsemane on Thursday of Holy Week, when at least one disciple brings along a sword.

Not all protests in Israel were violent. On a number of occasions, the same Jewish zeal found a nonviolent expression. The Jewish historian Josephus tells of an incident in which the Roman prefect Pontius Pilate had

Roman standards bearing the image of Caesar brought
into the city of Jerusalem.[4] This violated the Jewish law
prohibiting graven images—especially when they were
of a foreign conqueror who rocked titles such as "Son of
God." The protestors went to Pilate's home in Caesarea
and lay prostrate on the ground for five days. On the sixth
day, Pilate called the protestors together under the pre-
tense of giving a reply, only to have them surrounded by
his soldiers with their swords drawn. When they refused
to relent even under the threat of death, Pilate relented
and removed Caesar's standards from Jerusalem.

This definitely puts "In
God We Trust" in a
different perspective.

THE ACOLYTE

Thanks to the Dead Sea Scrolls at Qumran, we've
recently learned a lot about the Essenes. This discovery
has really helped fill out our picture of Jesus and John the
Baptist—and the vibe of apocalyptic Judaism in general.
The Essenes were an apocalyptic sect of Jewish dissent-
ers. They saw themselves as the only true practitioners of
Judaism, so they set up an alternative community in the
desert, practiced strict separation from the rest of Israel,
and engaged in intense religious ritual. They were monkish.[5] Their critique of the temple was harsh, going so far
as to turn baptism, a traditional act of ceremonial cleansing, into a substitute for temple worship—for them, baptism served as the remission of sin. Just imagine a huddle
of holy rollers hiding from all the sinners, planning for

war, and studying end-time Bible charts—except instead of finding it on a Texas public access channel, you had to drive out into the desert.

The Essenes had been around for over a hundred years before Herod the Great's three sons ended up in charge of Israel. By that point, their apocalyptic fervor and political critique had gained energy. They were anticipating a coming divine judgment of the present evil age. This imminent hope also included the coming of *two* messiahs: one to lead God's war of judgment on the present age and another to purify the temple for God. The Qumran community took this coming battle literally, including training and preparation for war in their daily routine. They were hardcore—not unlike the conspiracy survivalists who prepared for Y2K.

THE ACOLYTE

Why do religious groups love divine destruction so much?

Historians often highlight the similarities between John the Baptist and the Essenes. Both were centered on an apocalyptic message that challenged those in Israel to leave normal life behind and head out to the desert to get baptized so they'd be right with God on Judgment Day; both anticipated a messiah; and both were critics of Herod and the temple.

But of all the theo-political factions, the Pharisees were by far the most popular and the largest. They were primarily located in rural areas and focused on preserving

Jewish identity through study and through keeping the laws of Torah. Unlike the Sadducees, who recognized the written Torah alone as authoritative, the Pharisees also recognized the *oral* Torah, which was passed down from rabbi to rabbi for generations. They built an entire community around the text; discussion and even contentious debates became an integral part of the Pharisees' way of practicing Judaism. In the Gospels, the Pharisees often appear as Jesus' most venomous group of detractors, but their arguments over interpretations of Torah were a normal practice of theirs. They affirmed a belief in an afterlife, made strenuous ethical demands on their followers, and were critical of the leaders in Jerusalem. In other words, they were a lot like Jesus. Or maybe it's Jesus who was a lot like them.

Kind of like warring factions in a church. They think they are enemies, but both groups pick that church over all the others in town.

THE BISHOP

By ignoring this historical context, Christians have made a big mistake. They have often turned an internal debate between Jesus and the Pharisees over interpretations of their holy text into a battle between Christianity and Judaism. After Rome destroyed the temple in 70 CE, three different things happened that facilitated the parting of the ways between Judaism and Christianity. First, the temple itself, which brought most of these factions together on holidays, no longer existed.

Second, with no temple for Judaism or Christianity, both became text-centered religions. The destruction of the temple was like an earthquake that knocked down all the houses in the neighborhood except those of the Pharisees and the early Christians. Without the temple, the communities began to go their separate ways. The Pharisees, who were the progenitors of the Rabbinic Judaism we know today, began compiling the oral Torah, a collection of biblical interpretations, into the Talmud, and the early Christian communities began writing the Gospels and collecting Paul's letters.

THE DEACON

The destruction of the Temple was the first-century version of 9/11.

Speaking of Paul, the third reason that Judaism and Christianity ended up parting ways was his success. Numerically, the church came to be dominated more and more by gentiles—individuals who not only weren't Jewish, but before joining hadn't even been interested in the God of Abraham. The original disciples in Jerusalem weren't so sure about Paul's version of the gospel, but it's hard to argue with the effectiveness of a mission strategy that didn't require new Christians to convert to Judaism first. If I can brag for a minute, I'm a pretty good preacher, and I've been known to rock a revival invitation when necessary. But if, "with every head bowed and every eye closed," I first had to check whether all the fellas ask-ing Jesus into their heart were circumcised, I'm confident my batting average would take a dive. Paul removed this hurdle, and the church grew more quickly by conversion than Judaism could.

The important thing to understand here is just how much the religious landscape was changing so close to the birth of the church. And I'm just saying, it's likely that Jesus rocked a "Moses Is My Homeboy" foam mesh trucker hat.

Jesus Questers

Unlike the Holy Grail, Jesus of Nazareth was real and historical—that's something scholars agree about. We actually have more evidence for the existence of Jesus than any other Jew in the first century. Of course, there isn't much evidence for any particular person back then, and the information we do have is about a rather short period of time—Jesus' approximately three-year itinerant min-istry. In addition, all the sources have an agenda: they are Gospels about what God was doing in Jesus.

While scholars use the Gospels as sources, they're not committed to the theological framework of the authors. When historians talk about the "historical Jesus," they're referring to the best attempts at reconstructing the actual historical person, Jesus of Nazareth. The "quest for the his-torical Jesus" has gone on for a couple of centuries now—scholars say we're in currently in the "Third Quest"—and a pattern has developed that looks something like this: new evidence is discovered and consequently the "his-torical Jesus" is reconstructed and debated all over again.

Jesus-questers take the most secure facts about Jesus, place them in our growing awareness of his historical context, and then filter the biblical texts back through in order to extract the biases of the post-Easter church. This is why the destruction of the temple and the rise of the gentiles have been so theologically significant. They help us better understand both Jesus and the church.

There are as many historical Jesuses as there are Jesus-questers. The items that almost everyone agrees on are few but important. First, Jesus was obsessed with the kingdom of God, its presence, its coming, and the call to get on board. (What exactly Jesus thought the kingdom was, however, is less clear because he was appropriating a collection of common images and expectations within apocalyptic Judaism. So, for example, differentiating his own take on the kingdom from that of John the Baptist isn't easy.)

Second, scholars are confident that Jesus wanted to rescue Israel from its corrupt leadership and Roman occupation. Most scholars insist that he did have twelve disciples, who functioned symbolically as the twelve tribes of Israel, and that the disciples themselves took Jesus' message of restoration literally enough to ask about their own place in it.[6]

The third consensus among historians surrounds the end of Jesus' life: during his last week he provoked enough attention from the Roman leadership that he was deemed a political threat and crucified. Some scholars point toward the triumphal entry into Jerusalem, others to the cleansing of the temple, and still others to his public condemnation of the ruling elites. Whatever the reason, his ministry and message resulted in his execution. Neither the Jewish people nor all their leadership had Jesus killed. He was not crucified by a religion or an ethnic group but rather by the theo-political powers of the day.

The cooperation of religion and politics in the death of Jesus calls us to regularly examine ourselves as a church.

THE BISHOP

Lastly, there is a strong consensus among scholars that as part of his kingdom ministry, Jesus spoke in parables, was known to be a healer, and taught a spirituality centered on his understanding of God as *Abba*, Father. While other first-century Jewish prophets also preached about the kingdom of God and had public healing ministries, Jesus' emphasis on God as divine parent was unique. Here's what's hard to grasp: all those dynamics he had in common with other teachers can be understood many different ways. Historians continue to argue about them, but short of Jesus returning again to clarify things, their answers are rarely satisfying for most Christians. I think that's a good thing. After all, Paul said, "Even though we once knew Christ from a human point of view, we know him no longer in that way." The reason is simple: for Christians, the story of Jesus did not end with his death.[7]

Beyond these few things they are confident about, historians also work to evaluate the rest of the content in the Gospels and a few extrabiblical sources. The Gospels themselves share another feature in common—belief in the resurrection of Jesus from the dead. But historians cannot demonstrate the historical veracity of Jesus' resurrection (or anyone else's, for that matter). That's not how history works. At the very least, historians—whether Christian, Jewish, or atheist—can deduce that the earliest disciples both attested to and lived as if they had had an experience of a Jesus who was raised from the dead. But the question remains: Can you digest all of this historical speculation about Jesus and still have faith in him?

THE ACOLYTE

Great question. I also wonder how you can really distinguish the historical Jesus from the divine Jesus.

When Faith and History Collide

Some Christians fear historical investigation into the life and times of Jesus in the same way a Young Earth creationist fears Darwin. When I first got into historical Jesus studies in college, I went to a public lecture by a famous New Testament scholar who specializes in scaring Bible Belt literalists out of their Sunday certitude. It wasn't too long after the tragic events of September 11, 2001—the drumbeat for war was raging, nationalism was on the rise, and American religious superiority was assumed by the masses. I don't remember him touching current events at all, but he gave a powerful lecture on Jesus' understanding of the kingdom of God, its alternative economics, opposition to violence, and radical openness to the other and on Jesus' insistence that genuine hope was in what God was doing and not what those in power were doing. I was moved and challenged by the time the Q&A started, but there was an evangelical pastor in the crowd who was not amused. Not at all.

The question from the clergyman sounded more like a sermonette or a screed. He began with an apology, "I am sorry so many Bible-believing Christians were forced to listen to your academic gobbledygook. Why don't you just come out and say it? Tell us your opinion straight up and stop using big words, pictures of stuff someone dug up in the desert, and stories about a bunch of false messiahs in Jesus' day."

The scholar responded like he had handled this before and said with just a hint of a smirk, "I am glad to try to be clear with you—just tell me the part you missed in the form of a question."

"Well," the pastor responded, "let's say your Jesus was president of America and was deciding what the righteous and just thing to do is with all these Muslim terrorists, murderers, and the like. Do you want me to believe that he wouldn't bomb the hell out of them and protect the God-given freedoms we enjoy here in this blessed nation of ours?"

"Correct."

There was a significant pause as the rest of the room uncomfortably connected the dots.

Then the historian spoke again, "I wish I had a good parable for you. You see this is the kind of conversation Jesus was so good at. He would have answered your question with a story. The crowd would have loved it. It would have got you talking on the way home, and then that Trojan horse would open up and all the privilege and power being protected in your question would be under attack. But I am sure we both agree that I'm not Jesus, so I am stuck being direct. So here it is. Jesus would *never* be elected president because he refused to bow his knee to Satan during his wilderness temptation, and he constantly identified himself with the outcast and the suffering. I am confident Jesus would have mourned with all those who mourned after 9/11, but I am equally confident he would be praying that our loss and fear not become cancerous and lead to war. After all, now that we know who our enemies are, we know just who Jesus has commanded us to love."

The pastor was not deterred. He asked a follow-up: "Figured you'd say as much. One more question—this one's a bit more important. You've obviously read the Bible a bunch even if it never sticks. What do you say of Jesus Christ? Is he mad, bad, or just who he said he was?"

THE ACOLYTE

What do people hope to accomplish by being inhospitable turds in public for Jesus?

"Wonderful! Usually I get this question from someone who failed to notice that Jesus doesn't actually call himself God. Some of my students, not as astute as you, like to say he's either mad—you know, insane—bad, because he lied, or God even though he never claimed it for himself. I think he was who he said he was and more.

"Believe it or not, I am a Christian. Not because I can demonstrate historically that Jesus knew he was the eternal Son of God and a person of the Trinity, but because, like the earliest disciples, I have encountered God through this radical Jewish prophet who may have thought the world was about to end. As a historian, I'm interested in who Jesus thought he was, but I have faith that God was doing much more in him. Since I believe God was being revealed in Jesus, the simple fact that he took sides with the poor and oppressed of his day means that I can't ignore it, and as a disciple I have to try and do the same today. That's what I do with my life. I am a scholar but I am also a follower of Jesus. They go hand in hand for me, even though they are not the same."

That evening my roommate and I talked at the nearby Waffle House until the sun came up. We debated the relationship of our allegiances to our country and to

---

True or False: Waffle House brings the people together.

THE DEACON

---

our Lord. It was a completely new conversation for both of us. We were uncomfortable and unsure of what it all meant, but we did realize that way more was going on in Jesus than we had previously thought. As the year went by, we passed copies of books by Marcus Borg, N. T. Wright, E. P. Sanders, Neil Elliott, Paula Fredriksen, and more between us, returning again and again to this mysterious historical figure who was—and is—much more than a historical fascination.

This experience strengthened my conviction that the study of the historical Jesus can't be ignored *on purely Christian grounds.* For one thing, the content of the Gospels includes historical affirmations. Ignoring the quest for the historical Jesus means we could be cutting ourselves off from greater understanding of what we call most dear—Jesus! And for another thing, the doctrine of the incarnation raises the historical question, for it insists that God was actually present in Jesus of Nazareth. Snubbing the historical Jesus is a contemporary version of an early church heresy called Docetism, which separated the divinity of Jesus from the historical person. Christians have insisted throughout our history that it was *through* Jesus of Nazareth, and not some ideas occasioned by or about him, that God sought us out. We have also confessed that the story of Jesus did not end at the cross but that he lives and is present in and through the life of the church.

I cannot overstate that, for Christians, it's essential that the Jesus who died cross-dead is the same one we call the Christ. We will always say *more* about Jesus than the historians—to say less than they do is a big problem.

If you talk to people about Jesus a lot, like I do for the podcast, and especially if you talk to people with PhDs in Jesus stuff, you might get the impression that there are two camps. One wants only to talk about Jesus as we knew him before the seventeenth century—all divine Son of God, no Jew. The other will only consider data since the seventeenth century—all historical Jew, no miracles, divinity, or mystery at all. Each camp is only getting half the story because Jesus is way more awesome than they realize.

Abba Says, "Drop the G"

I remember the first time I talked to someone who really had no clue about Jesus—she knew nothing about him beyond his birth story, death story, and accompanying holidays. Her name was Angela, and she was a college sophomore sent to interview a minister from the religion she was least attracted to. That's probably not how it was written in the syllabus, but it definitely made for a conversation I wasn't going to pass up.

We met at the Coffee Cartel, my local shop, and, after giving a brief apology up front, she was all business. "Look, I don't know much about Christianity," she began. "Never really liked any of the Christians I've met. My family is theoretically Jewish, practically atheist; I do yoga, eat meat, and am more of a religious free agent. That said, I am not really considering Christianity, so don't take it personally if, at least in your mind, I leave this interview still going to hell or something."

I said I'd would stick with the "something" and do my best to avoid converting her (even though the ocean was just a block away, convenient for a baptism). She had no idea what that was, so I laughed and we began.

THE ELDER

Is anyone surprised this story took place in Southern California?

"So, I am only supposed to ask you three questions. Then I can ask follow-ups and stuff. I was thinking of asking why Christians think God made so many people to go to hell, what you think happens when you pray, and what's so bad about being gay. But, if you want, just tell me some better questions and I'll ask those. I just googled 'Christians,' and those seemed like popular topics."

I was so impressed that Angela set it up this way, actually asking me to suggest questions, that I proposed she just ask me one: "Why are you so into Jesus?" We ended up talking about that question for two hours.

A month later, I got an email thanking me for the conversation and the coffee. In it she mentioned being truly surprised to learn about Jesus and his radical mission and vision for the world. She had no idea he was so controversial or inspiring. She went on to describe the response of her class to a presentation about her interview. A couple of her peers were Christians and didn't believe that I could be a real Christian minister. (Those same individuals were reportedly very clear about how much anger God has for sinners, how Jesus took God's punishment for all who believe in him, and how Jesus is basically a white upper-middle-class Republican who loves guns, straight people's wedding cakes, and unnecessary wars in Muslim countries.) Angela and the professor were both taken aback that the students responded to her presentation with such animosity. After all, she was simply reporting on her interview.

What I loved the most in her email was her response to those students. The professor suggested that she ignore the commentary unless she had an idea about how I might respond to the allegations. Angela decided to read her favorite part of the interview, in which I explained why Jesus was awesome:

> If there's a God, She's a mystery. As a Christian, I believe that mystery is revealed most clearly to me in Jesus. Whenever I hear someone—even Christians—talking about God and they seem to be full of hate, judgment, and anger, I think of Jesus on the cross who said, "Forgive them, for they know not what they do." If that's the mystery being revealed, then any image of God needs to match it or you should ditch it. God has to be at least as nice as Jesus. If not, we're ignoring the most important part.

That concluded her presentation, but it was just the beginning of our coffee house chats.

Awesome is an overused word. I use it all the time for things like the world's greatest pale ale (Drake's 1500) or Bob Dylan and The Band's *Before the Flood* live album—specifically the version of "Up on Cripple Creek." But when it comes to Jesus, I think this word—defined by the dictionary as an intense level of unsurpassed inspiration—is perfectly appropriate. In my conversations with Angela, I tried to explain that part of the reason Christians misunderstand Jesus is that they have a habit of interpreting Jesus' significance apart from Jesus' own mission and vision of God. When that happens, Christians turn the call to discipleship into an escape—an escape from the troubles of this world or an escape from eternal punishment. We spiritualize Jesus' concern for the outcast and the poor, and we end up ignoring Jesus' obsession with bringing the party. Looking at some of the broad features of Jesus' ministry in their historical context will help us home in on the awesome sauce that he brought.

The Kingdom of God

Jesus has a bunch of titles. People could legitimately call him all sorts of things: preacher, teacher, outlaw, healer,

THE ELDER

Jesus was kind of like the Manny Pacquiao of rabbis.

rebel, wanderer. If Jesus ever made an appearance on cable news and they had to use just one label in that little box at the bottom of the screen, it might read, "Jesus of Nazareth, proclaimer of God's kingdom." Nothing occupied Jesus' mind, mouth, and ministry like the kingdom of God. In fact, to understand what Jesus said, did, and even suffered, the kingdom of God is the single necessary point of reference. He talked about it all the time, and, I would argue, everything he did was a testament to it.

Yet despite Jesus' obsession with the kingdom, the church has remained aloof from kingdom concerns. Partly this is because of just how hardcore the kingdom of God is. Taking it seriously is hazardous to running a well-oiled institution like the church. Perhaps even more alarming is the sheer lack of awareness of the kingdom focus of Jesus'

I always thought preachers who talk about the kingdom too much were just Democrats.

THE ELDER

---

ministry among most churchgoers. If the only people who have a rich understanding of the kingdom of God are the few with graduate degrees in religion, then we shouldn't be surprised that the church isn't attentive to it.

The idea of the kingdom of God was not born in a vacuum. It's a product of Judaism's commitment to the goodness of God and to monotheism. Part of being a monotheist who insists that the one good God made this one good world is asking why there's so much unjust suffering and evil in it. The kingdom of God is an answer to this question, emphasizing God's actions to fulfill God's promises. Within the Hebrew Scriptures, there's no clear answer to the problem of evil, but the people of Israel insist that their God will remain faithful and that, despite evidence to the contrary, God is good.

The violent history of humanity poses a serious challenge to the character and sovereignty of God, even turning a question about the essence of God into one about the existence of God. At some point, the corpses of the God-abandoned add up, and you not only have to ask who God is but also if God is.

It's not until the very end of the Hebrew Scriptures that an apocalyptic answer to this question emerges. It's all over the book of Daniel, but, apart from that, there are very few passages that anticipate these questions within Judaism. For the purposes of more fully understanding Jesus' vision of the kingdom of God, we need to note two features. First, God's eschatological coming is primarily about God's activity. That is, God will finally fulfill God's promise of restoration. Second, the arrival of this new age will include a cataclysmic encounter with the current one wherein God's hopes break into a seemingly hopeless present age.

THE ACOLYTE

So what we call the problem of evil is actually a challenge to the character of God?

A helpful way to see how Jesus inherits this "eschatological hope," which is just a nerdy way to say "the hope about God's final judgment and justice being accomplished," is to contrast his own hope with that of John the Baptist. John stood outside the dominant society, insisting people come out to the river to be baptized and get right with God. John preached that God's wrathful judgment was on the horizon and the impotence of the temple to prepare the people for that wrath. From the Jewish historian Josephus, we learn that John did not baptize everyone who came out to the desert—he only administered baptism after the penitent's skin was sagging from intense fasting and contrition.

In contrast, Jesus did not stand outside of Jerusalem, lobbing prophetic judgments over the city walls. He did not wait for the sinners to take the initiative to fast and seek repentance. Jesus went from town to town announcing the kingdom of God, forgiving sin, healing the broken, and throwing parties. His message of the kingdom was for everyone, and, more importantly, he took the message to the people. The Gospel of Mark gives us a one-sentence sermon that summarizes Jesus' proclamation: "The time is fulfilled, and the kingdom of God has come near; repent, and believe in the good news."[1]

For Jesus, God's coming was good news, especially for the poor, outcast, and oppressed. He not only proclaimed the message of the kingdom, but he actualized it, he inaugurated it, he made it real. In the ministry of Jesus, God's coming rule came so close and became so intimate that God came to be best understood as Abba. Not only that, but the coming restoration of creation was no longer in some promised future but rather in a future erupting into the present. Unlike other prophets, Jesus did not foretell God's coming kingdom as a complete break with the present world. Instead, through the work of Jesus, the world as it is was being introduced to the world as it will be when the kingdom comes on earth as it is in heaven. And this coming has implications for religion, politics, and community.

The Kingdom and Religion

Jesus' message was seriously put to the test after he died. I mean, he'd been walking the countryside, promising everybody with ears to hear that God was doing a new thing. Then he went and got killed by an empire, just like so many religious prophets before him and since. How was his death any different than theirs? And how was his message any truer than theirs?

The early church had a quandary. How was God present in Jesus of Nazareth when he walked around Palestine? And how did Jesus continue to mediate God's presence even after his death, resurrection, and ascension? Their largest source of data for this question was Jesus' ministry, and the most controversial act of Jesus' own ministry was his forgiveness of sin. No other prophet claimed the authority to forgive sin, but Jesus did. His religious opponents were deeply disturbed by the hubris of such a claim when that job was God's alone.

If Jesus simply proclaimed the coming of God's kingdom but did not bring it about, then his forgiveness of sin makes no sense. The Temple system was already in place to manage the sins of the people and ensure forgiveness— that's the sacrificial system we read about in Leviticus and elsewhere in the Hebrew Bible. But Jesus' addition was the dawning of the kingdom of God and a growing intimacy between God and the people. This was Jesus' new twist on the old message.

Nothing could make this clearer than when Jesus called God "Abba." This familial-divine address emphasized the nearness and availability of God. Not only was this an intimate relational term for Jesus' own relationship with God, but it also sits at the heart of the spirituality he taught his own disciples. "When you pray," Jesus said, "pray like this: Our Father."[2] In Jesus' own embrace of divine intimacy with God and his ability to take forgiveness to the streets, the kingdom was not only coming, it was *arriving now.*

Today, the image of God as Abba/Father doesn't communicate the radical intimacy that it did for Jesus' own disciples. For some, troubling histories with their own fathers tarnish this image. And for many, myself included, exclusively masculine pronouns for God are deeply problematic for theological reasons, having justified patriarchy and hierarchy in what should be an egalitarian community. Jesus had no problem using both masculine and feminine imagery for God. In the span of just one chapter of Luke, God is described as a shepherd searching for his lost sheep, a woman looking in every nook and cranny of her house for her lost coin, and a father eagerly waiting to throw a party for his lost son. The key to thinking of God as Abba/Father is not to let the language distract us from the good news that the God who made the world knows our names, knows our faces, and cares for us. This was the radical insight that Jesus introduced.

God is our father, and she loves us dearly.

Yes, God is our mother, and he will not let us go.[3]

Does "God is our MoFa" work?

THE DEACON

Although the parental image exists within the Hebrew Scriptures and so was available to Jesus, the primacy Jesus placed on that image, over against the other dominant depictions of God, such as king and judge, is possibly the most radical aspect of his teaching about God. For when the King is our Abba, we are so much more than expendable serfs under the command of the cosmic ruler. We are Abba's heirs. We are royalty. Likewise, when we enter the courtroom of the celestial judge, we may think we are on trial for high crimes against the law of God, but when Abba is Judge there are no charges; it's always an adoption proceeding.

THE BISHOP

Churches that fight over gendered language about God tend to be the ones that ignore another 100-plus other images as well. Patriarchy hides in the poetic impoverishment.

This message was radical, but remember: Jesus was not talking about himself. He was talking about God. Although the new reality of the relationship between us and God was mediated by Jesus when he said things like "Your sins are forgiven, take up your mat and walk" or "Repent and believe," it was always about *God's kingdom* and not himself.

The Kingdom and Community

One of the things that I love most about *Homebrewed Christianity* is that it's a lot more than a podcast. It's a

One of the things I love about Homebrewed Christianity is that it's given me a reason to stay Christian. Also, the beer helps.

THE DEACON

community. These days, we've even structured it like a church community, with deacons, elders, bishops, and more. When listeners call in to the "Speak Pipe" with their thoughts and questions, it's clear that we're all in this together. And when I travel, I meet people all over who are part of the HBC posse. There's something about searching for meaning in life that is best done with other people.

When we consider the life and ministry of Jesus, it's important to notice the centrality of community. Jesus may have been the Messiah, but he did not take up his vocation alone. He was deliberately in the community of his disciples. The very heart of Jesus' teaching centers on the practice, ethics, and mission of this community that he initiated with the disciples and evolved into the church. From the Sermon on the Mount to the sending of his disciples, the kingdom of God works through people in relationship.

Take Jesus' teaching on forgiveness. He insisted that there was a relationship between the forgiveness we receive from God and the forgiveness we offer to one another. Forgive about worshipping or even sleeping when a relationship is strained or fractured, Jesus said. Instead, work toward reconciliation. When he was asked how many times someone should forgive another person, Jesus famously said, "Not seven times, but, I tell you, seventy times seven."[4] The economy of forgiveness that the kingdom of God establishes in the community of disciples is one that doesn't keep score. Instead, the community seeks reconciliation in *every* instance, just as God seeks reconciliation.

This attention to the character of the community and the cultivation of a new way to do religion occupies much of Jesus' preaching. Once, when I taught a confirmation class of high school students, we spent three months on the Sermon on the Mount. Each month, we created an experiment around one of Jesus' teachings. It's always amazing what happens when you actually do what Jesus asked his disciples to do: to forgive without counting, to pray for your enemies (including annoying and overprotective parents dead set against you becoming an adult or having any fun in the process), and even to refuse to participate in any conversations of judgment. One of my students came up with a metaphor that has stuck with me. He said that Jesus did not come to give the disciples the perfect update to the religious operating system or to install an invincible antivirus program; the kingdom of God brings an entirely new operating system.

THE DEACON

But you didn't answer the important question: Was it a PC or a Mac?

This new operating system of the kingdom remembers the biblical commands against adultery and for loving your neighbor, but it intensifies them in a specific way. When Jesus says, "But I say that everyone who looks at a woman with lust has already committed adultery with her in his heart" and "Love your enemies and pray for those who persecute you," he is insisting that every person retains the dignity appropriate to a child of God, created in God's image.[5] It's not enough to avoid hooking up with someone else's partner. No, the point is to become a person who doesn't turn others into objects of your desire. Likewise, the activity of deciding who is your neighbor and who is your enemy misunderstands the command to love your neighbor. To love and pray for your enemies is actually something much more radical: destroying the label of enemy altogether.

Politics and the Kingdom

Recently, historical Jesus scholars have brought to our attention the political ramifications of Jesus' kingdom vision. Working backward from his death on a Roman cross with the title "King of the Jews" hanging over his head, it's a bit surprising how we missed it until now.

The assumption Jesus shared with all the apocalyptic prophets is that the world as God wants it to be must replace the world as it is, including the reigning powers of the day. This was enacted by the coming of the kingdom of God. In Jesus' time, the word *kingdom* had unmistakable political connotations. The world was full of kings (and emperors and pharaohs) and kingdoms (and empires), and Jesus' insistence that God's kingdom was on earth as it is in heaven pushed against anyone's temptation to overly spiritualize his message. When you think about

THE ACOLYTE

Any good ideas about how to make this happen? I'd be interested in that kind of Christianity.

the nature of competing kingdoms, it isn't surprising that Pilate had Jesus put to death on behalf of Caesar, even if it sounds like news to many modern-day Christians.

Modern New Testament scholars say events surrounding the last week of Jesus' life were touchstones for understanding both the political implications of his ministry and the actual actions that precipitated his death. For example, Jesus' entry into Jerusalem on a donkey with the crowd of supporters celebrating his arrival could not have gone unnoticed. After all, Jesus and thousands of other travelers were coming into Jerusalem to celebrate the Passover, a festival that memorialized God's liberation of the Israelites. It doesn't take a genius to put two and two together and notice that Jesus' display had political overtones, especially since Pilate had earlier paraded into town on a warhorse with centurions around him. As if the entry were not clear enough, Jesus then went to the temple and cleared out the merchants. Given the cooperation between the temple's leadership and the Roman occupiers, interrupting the monetization of their infidelity was quite direct.

The contrast between the kingdom of God and the empire of Caesar could not have been starker than in the

Does the stark nature of the contrast between the kingdom of God and the political powers of our day remain? If so, it doesn't get much air time on Sundays.

THE ACOLYTE

consequence of his political provocation. In the humiliation and execution of Jesus, we see two very different images of power. Rome and its emperor Caesar, son of God, extended and preserved his kingdom through violence. In contrast, the kingdom of God came not by cross building but by cross bearing; it was not coercive but persuasive, not top-down power but bottom-up. God's victory was not consummated through the annihilation of God's enemies but by the transformation of those enemies into friends. God made this possible by turning the cross

I think it is important when raising such heated issues like politics to remember that God's end goal is friendship and reconciliation.

THE BISHOP

from a symbol of *us-versus-them* power into a *God-is-with-us* power.

The Kingdom Catch

I could write an entire book about my love of Jesus and the kingdom he proclaimed. But to end this chapter, I want to highlight a predicament that contemporary scholars and theologians have when discussing the kingdom of God. The problem is its name. You could put it this way: should we continue to translate *basilea theou* as the "kingdom of God"?

In one sense, it's a perfect, literal translation. But our contemporary situation no longer includes kingdoms and kings. Some theologians suggest that retaining the hierarchical image of the kingdom and the patriarchal image of a king fails to do justice to the idea as it is described by and embodied in Jesus. In his own context, Jesus' language was clearly subversive, giving an upside-down image of the meaning of *king* and *kingdom*. Today, there's a legitimate concern that by preserving dated language, we miss the real meaning and instead appropriate these terms on behalf of contemporary perversions of power. The church has for too long been a harbor for patriarchy and has all too often been subservient to and cooperative with the reigning powers of the world. It may be time to change the language.

This predicament has inspired a collection of alternative translations of *basilea theou*. For example, some translate it as the *realm of God*, the *reign of God*, or the *commonwealth of God*. Others attempt to communicate Jesus' positive vision of the kingdom by using alternative imagery such as *God's project*, the *ecosystem of God*, or the *God movement*.

Once, I was present for a conversation between three of the most influential living theologians: John Cobb,

Philip Clayton, and Catherine Keller. Cobb thought the cornucopia of options was helpful descriptively, but within the text itself he opted to keep it in Greek, leaving *basilea theou* untranslated. Keller argued that the promissory and prophetic power of the *basilea theou* should be made clear in the translation of the text. Given our present situation within the *Pax Americana* (an expression that compares the empire of the United States to that of Rome in Jesus' day), she thought the phrase *commonwealth of God* brought the political and economic implications to the fore for today's world. Clayton insisted that the most appropriate translation remains the *kingdom of God*, not because we should ignore the patriarchy and hierarchy tied up in the image but because Jesus used the phrase to befuddle and challenge those very same powers in his own day. Clayton said that the kingdom of God both then and now should be defined by Jesus' enactment of it. When it is, it will not be tamed.

I find all three arguments persuasive. Each insists that the heart of Jesus' message is powerful, challenging, and integral to the life of the church. The key is to allow the historical Jesus and the radical nature of his own mission on behalf of God to disturb and provoke us today.

As a minister, I have challenged my congregation by dropping the *G* out of kingdom. I can preach an entire sermon, and only a few people with ears to hear will notice the absence of that one letter. When they ask why I preached "kin-dom" instead of kingdom, I point out that when you remove the letter *G*, you take both the phallus and the crown out of the kingdom. After all, that is how Jesus rolled.

THE ELDER

The idea of a minister saying "phallus" is disturbing.

Is the Kin-dom Still Present and Coming?

One of the most exciting things I get to do is to help put together conferences on a variety of religious and theological topics. As an organizer, I'm like a theological matchmaker, hoping to get the right people in conversation on the right topic so that the imaginative sparks can fly. When the conference speakers range from scholars to ministers to activists to denominational executives, there is sometimes healthy cross-pollination, and sometimes participants politely talk past one another. On occasion, however, there's been real-deal heat!

I once moderated a session with two featured speakers, one a famous historical Jesus scholar and the other a creative community organizer. I put them together because they're both notorious for taking everything back to Jesus' preaching about the kingdom. They even both shared the same mantra: "the kingdom of God is both present and coming, so join in." Both speakers were on point, getting laughs and even a few amens from the crowd. And each was visibly enjoying what the other was saying. It was one of the few times I thought to myself, "Tripp, you were wise to pair these two together."

At the end of the session, I asked them questions that they answered in tandem. As we went along, I wove in questions from the audience, sent in on notecards or posted to Twitter. The experience felt like a rehearsed tag-team sermon, with the two singing different verses of the same song. Then an important yet hidden division came to the fore, the relationship of God to the kingdom.

"Is the kingdom of God still present and coming after the sun swallows our planet?" read the last question of the session. Without hesitation, the Jesus scholar answered with confidence, "Of course not. If humanity is dead and gone, who is here to bring the kingdom into being? The question of the kingdom should be asked in a sociopolitical context and not as science fiction. I don't intend to sound dismissive, but you could have just as easily asked me where Jesus went when he ascended into heaven." His conversation partner passed on the question, as the more progressive people in the room clapped with gusto for the answer.

I still don't get why
Jesus Seminar fans clap
their hands about NOT
believing something. Ugh.

THE ELDER

Afterward, someone asked me, "What was up with his last answer? Where did that come from?" I said, "Well, once you've decided God can't say more than history permits, that answer makes perfect sense." She responded with the question that was running through the minds of many audience members, "Isn't that the whole point of the resurrection?"

THE BISHOP

Really? I think the clapping is for a church who made space not only for skeptics to be present but to even get the microphone.

The Resurrection and the Kin-dom

The reality is that after the resurrection, the early church inherited and continued Jesus' radical kin-dom mission. Today, even within the church, Jesus is often portrayed as benign and boring. Discussions about the kin-dom of God and the resurrection of Jesus have become debates about the afterlife and arguments over historical evidence. These conversations can be like chewing glass. More than that, they miss the entire point!

To understand the resurrection, you need to hear it as a proclamation about God's eschatological work. If Jesus understood God to be answering the cries of Israel for God's presence, then the cross of Jesus stands as testimony *against* God. The cross insists that the affirmation of life and vitality experienced in the kin-dom ministry of Jesus is negated in his death. The tomb of Christ is a symbol of closure to Jesus' mission and also to the coming God that he proclaimed.

This is why the kin-dom, which is already but not yet, hit more than a hiccup on the cross. If the kin-dom was God's answer and God's work, then, as Christ lay dead, he joined millions of corpses rightly protesting against this so-called good God. A Jesus who is not raised haunts more than the church. He's the ghost who spooks all dreams of liberation and the ghoul who feeds off the death of God. Said another way, God's essence and existence are inevitably at stake in the death and resurrection of Jesus.

To separate the kin-dom of God from the cross of Jesus is to misunderstand the purpose of the kin-dom alto-

---

Kin-don-inspired theologies of the cross and those without are

THE DEACON

so different I wonder if they are just different religions. If so, I can be a bit more tolerant of ignoring Jesus.

---

gether. Jesus was not suggesting new ideas about religion, community, or politics, as if these concepts could even be detached from each other and taken up later. Jesus was announcing and inaugurating God's response to the question of history, evil, and suffering. The kin-dom of God was not just about God conceptually, as if the concept of God needed clarification; it was about God's very essence and existence.

It was in light of this eschatological framework of the kin-dom that the early church sought to understand the resurrection of Jesus. When God raised Jesus from the dead, the apostles saw that event as the first fruits of God's promise, as the resurrection of Jesus, an individual person in history. This did not fit with the belief in general resurrection (that is, the idea that *everyone* would be raised at the end of time) that was common among apocalyptic Jews. It was the reaffirmation of life after its negation, the rupturing of death's closure and the revelation that Abba's kin-dom was still present and coming.

The resurrection must be seen as an eschatological event. It is a statement about the very nature and name of God. When the resurrection is turned into a debate about the biology of the postmortem Jesus, then we are belittling the early church's claim. The resurrection is more than just

---

THE ACOLYTE

If the resurrection is about God, then why argue with Bill Nye the Science Guy about it?

---

a statement about Jesus—it is a promise from God. This promise insists that the cross-bearer and the kin-dom he proclaimed will be God's final word to the cross-building powers of this world. When the resurrected Christ said to his disciples, "As the Father sent me, so I send you," it was anything but boring and benign.[6] Jesus' mission was dangerous, exciting, and liberating, and ours is too.

Because God raised Jesus from the dead, the church continues to proclaim that this kin-dom is *present and coming*. We are sent to join in its arrival, but we are not what's coming. Christianity without a kin-dom leaves Jesus behind. Christianity without a cross is glib and naive. But, just as important, Christianity without the resurrection has a kin-dom without a future, a cross that is final, and a God whose essence and existence aren't spoken for.

The eschatological Judaism of Jesus' context informed not only his own identity and mission but also the church's understanding of it. Both the kin-dom and the resurrection are concepts thoroughly forged in the history of Israel and necessitated by Rome's occupation. They cannot be understood apart from each other. While denying the divinity of Jesus doesn't make him a liar, denying the eschatological nature of the resurrection does make God one.

Reading the Gospels Heresy-Free

One of the things about my upbringing I'm most grateful for is the love of Scripture that my parents gave me. I remember thinking I had finally arrived when I was able to read the Bible and pray by myself before bed. I loved it! I read the Bible every night in my bed, so proud of my accomplishment.

Then, during Holy Week when I was in fourth grade, I discovered that my Bible was broken.

I had decided to read all four Gospel accounts of Jesus' final week. As a dutiful student of the Bible, I remember charting out just what Jesus did, when it happened, and how it went down. But I found a mistake in the Bible my parents had given me. More than one, in fact. The Gospels didn't all have Jesus dying on the same day! Plus, they contained inconsistencies about what Jesus said from the cross, who was there when he died, who was at the tomb, and even details about the resurrected Christ—in one, he can go through walls; in another, he's eating fish. You would think a good editor would have noticed these glaring contradictions.

THE ACOLYTE

Pause. I need to reread
those stories.

When I expressed my dismay to my dad, he assured me that my Bible was not broken and that the Gospels I read are the same four Gospels found in every Bible. He told me that each of the four Gospels had its own unique account of what God did in Jesus. He explained it to me by likening the four Gospels to the four members of our family explaining how amazing our trip to Florida was. We would each mention spring training baseball, good times at Disney World, a nighttime spaceship launch, and some great large-mouth bass fishing. But I would focus on the Vero Beach Dodger games, my brother on the Mets, and my dad on the Orioles and the size of Mark McGwire's forearms.

All of that is to say, the four of us had experienced the same trip to Florida, but we would each recount the trip differently. I bet when Mom reads this she'll tell me I've collapsed multiple trips to Florida into one, but that's OK because when the Fuller family went to Florida, we made serious memories. Now imagine that the four of us weren't actually present for everything that happened on the trip; instead, the stories were passed down orally for more than forty years and we used multiple sources when writing our accounts. Despite the glaring differences, the Fuller family archive includes all four versions—on purpose.

The Tatian Temptation

A number of people wrote down their accounts, and these gospels circulated among the churches. Eventually, the early church leaders debated which ones to include in the New Testament. In that time, there was a theologian named Tatian (c. 120–c. 180 CE) who could not handle the contradictions the testimonies offered. He created the first "harmony gospel," a single account of the life of Jesus in which there were no contradictions. It's called the *Diatessaron*, which is a pretty sweet name and literally means "out of four." For example, the Gospel of John has Jesus cleansing the temple at the beginning of his ministry and the other three have him doing it at the end, so Tatian's gospel depicts him doing it twice. This line of thinking eventually got Tatian condemned as a heretic, but he just could not trust the veracity of the gospel unless all the details lined up!

A lot of us are tempted to want Tatian's gospel: a nice and tidy account of Jesus that we can read and believe without question. Despite the popularity of the harmony

Too many want a childish faith rather than a child-like faith, and they never grow past it.

THE BISHOP

gospel, the church condemned it and instead chose to include the four Gospels we have today. And it turns out that having four Gospels actually serves an important purpose. Since Christians hold that the Word of God is Jesus Christ, not any single text, having these four testimonies to the Christ event keeps us from confusing the text with the person, the story with the experience, and the surface with the content.

The Gospels are a genre of literature. The authors intended to tell the story of Jesus, each in a very particular way. That doesn't mean they aren't trustworthy, but they definitely are not "objective history," a concept unknown in Jesus' day. Just as there's a difference in how you read the different sections of a newspaper—an editorial versus front-page news versus the comics—reading a Gospel requires a certain type of reading.

The evangelists—a term for the authors of the Gospels—were not telling the story of a dead Jesus, but of

---

THE ACOLYTE

I guess it's okay to use the term "evangelist" as long as you don't add "tel-" at the front of it.

---

the resurrected Christ. The communities that gave birth to these texts believed that God had raised Jesus from the dead. And, even more, the church had an ongoing relationship with the resurrected Christ, and they believed that Christ mediated the community's relationship to God. Telling the story of this resurrected Christ needed more than a simple biography. A Gospel is a multidimensional telling of the story of Jesus—a Jesus who has come to be known as the Christ.

Everything that happened in his ministry and even on the cross is known and interpreted in the Gospels in light of Jesus' *end*—the resurrection—which is also a new beginning. Think of it like a wedding toast given by a grooms-man. As the groom's friend for years, he knows the best and worst parts of the guy, but knowing that the history leads to this celebration, he tells the stories during the toast in a new way—in light of the ending. This retroactive realization that the Spirit of God was always at work in Christ gave the early church a new lens for reading the Hebrew Scriptures and telling the stories of Jesus. Doing this was not a sleight of hand or twisting of the truth, at least from their perspective, because they were bringing God's self-testimony in Christ to the fore. The cool thing about having four Gospels in the New Testament is that we get to hear four different theological tellings of the Jesus story.

One canon, many voices. One church, many testimonies. This is what faithful freedom looks like!

THE DEACON

Where should the story begin? If you asked most people how to start the story of Jesus, it'd be like a Christmas pageant at church: shepherds, angels, and wise men crammed into a stable, bowing before a glowing manger.

But here's the deal: the shepherds and wise men never met, Jesus and John the Baptist aren't really related, and there was no census that sent every conquered subject of Rome back to their ancestral home for tax purposes. And that verse in Isaiah about the "virgin conceiving" isn't even about the state of the woman's hymen. There's a bit more to it than that, but take a deep breath. The first time I read a distinguished Bible scholar writing about all of this, I took his book and threw it out of my bedroom window. Luckily, I managed to keep reading (a different author's book) and found out that the birth stories are still pretty sweet. Of course, you may miss just how awesome they are if you're

---

THE ELDER

Just ruin Christmas, why don't you? Next you're gonna tell me there's a real Santa, and I didn't have to buy so many presents.

---

hung up on the veracity of the Christmas pageant.

We're going to start with Mark, the first Gospel written—but you'll notice there's no baby in the manger. As we look at each, we will pay attention to how it gives an account of Jesus' beginning that coheres with the new beginning at the end. Follow that?

Mark

The earliest of the Gospels is Mark, written around 70 CE.[1] Mark is the shortest of all the Gospels and quickly gets to the point. There's no manger and no donkeys. Mark begins with a reference to the prophet Isaiah's call, "Prepare for the way of the Lord, make his paths straight."[2] This verse, which anticipates a new exodus, a return from exile, is what frames the ministry of John the Baptist and his expectation for the coming of another, greater prophet.

In Mark's version of Jesus' baptism, it's only Jesus who experiences the opening of the heavens, the Spirit's descent, and the voice from heaven. This word from heaven—"You are my Son, the Beloved; with you I am well pleased"[3]—identifies Jesus as God's son and echoes the anointing of both a new king and the people of Israel for the work of renewal.[4] From here, the Spirit drives Jesus out into the desert where he is tempted by Satan; then, after the arrest of John, Jesus begins his ministry. In just fifteen verses, Jesus has already started his ministry, announcing the kingdom of God as the renewal of Israel and calling disciples to join his endeavor.

For Mark, it's the descent of the Spirit and the anointing by the Father at Jesus' baptism that sets Jesus apart and launches his messianic mission. This is in contrast to Paul and the other Gospels because here there's no hint of a miraculous conception (as in Matthew and Luke), no preexistent status of the Christ (as in John), and no revelation of Jesus as God's son only after the resurrection (as in Paul).[5] In Mark, the story of Jesus always looks toward the

---

This wrecked me in seminary (in a good way). #sufferingservant

THE DEACON

cross, the expected confrontation between God's kingdom and the world. Jesus' prophetic intensity is consistently turned toward his disciples, insisting that they walk in the way of the Lord and give God's kingdom their ultimate allegiance. Jesus' pastoral concern for discipleship, a call to remain faithful in spite of the tumultuous situation, is primary. And remember, if scholars are correct that Mark was written around 70 CE, that corresponds with the destruction of the temple and the earth-shaking changes that followed, so faithfulness mattered.

Although the first verse of the Gospel reads, "The beginning of the good news of Jesus Christ, the Son of God," it's not until Jesus hangs dead on the cross that a centurion says, "Truly this man was the son of God."[6] Mark saw Jesus as the son of God in a *functional* sense, as the suffering servant-messiah of God's kingdom. This means that what most Christians think when they hear the phrase "Son of God"—the metaphysical connection between the Father and Son from all eternity—is not what Mark meant. For Mark, Jesus isn't a deity, come down to rescue humanity. Jesus is a suffering messiah, offering hope through a sacrificial life and death.

THE ACOLYTE

I had no idea there was such diversity and evolution about how to understand Jesus. How are we supposed to read the Gospels without a clue?

Here you might be tempted to start quoting other books of the New Testament, but pause for a second before you do. Isn't it refreshing to know that the Bible includes this much less robust affirmation of Jesus Christ? I know there have been times in my life when Mark's low Christology is all I could muster.[7] I know friends for whom Mark's testimony is much closer to their own than Paul's or John's is. If Mark is allowed in the canon, then my friends should be allowed in church.

Locating the Evangelist's Voice

As we turn to look at the Gospels of Matthew and Luke, we need to understand their relationship to Mark. These three are called the *Synoptic Gospels* because they share roughly the same narrative outline. Matthew and Luke were written after Mark and most likely relied on Mark and a hypothetical document of Jesus' sayings called "Q" in their construction. If you put all three Gospels on parallel timelines, you'll see that over 90 percent of Mark is in the other two, and Mark basically sets the narrative order for all three. If you subtract all the elements of Mark from Luke and Matthew, a bunch of sayings and parables of Jesus remain. Because the sayings in Luke and Matthew are similar, scholars have hypothesized that this material comes from a text we no longer have, and they've named this source "Q," short for the German word *Quelle*, meaning "source." (Nerdy, I know.)

When trying to get in the heads of Matthew and Luke, look at their unique material, such as the setting in which they place a saying. In these instances we see more of the author's hand and thus their unique theological witness to Christ. (More nerdiness: this is called *redaction criticism*.) Let's look then at the specific character of each evangelist's voice.

Matthew

The Gospel of Matthew was written about a decade after Mark and comes from a community of Jewish Christians. In this period, Judaism (post-temple) and Christianity (brand new) were becoming distinct from one another, and Matthew reflects this distancing. Matthew tells the story of Jesus with clear parallels to the life of Moses, symbolically saying that Jesus is the new Moses, come to liberate the people of Israel.

The Gospel itself centers around five long teachings of Jesus, hearkening back to the five books of Moses, and it begins with a genealogy that goes back to Abraham, runs through David, and includes four independent, powerful, and even scandalous women—Tamar, Ruth, Rahab, and Bathsheba. Here we get the first mention of Joseph and of Mary's virgin conception by the Spirit, but in Matthew almost the entire plot of the birth narrative comes through Joseph and his dreams. When Mary gave birth to Jesus, a star began to shine that drew the attention of some stargazing astrologers in the East who headed off to Judea to witness the birth of the new King.

Herod, the king of Jews, was perplexed when the Magi came calling. He sent them ahead to check things out, intent on killing the child if he turned out to be a threat. These pagan astrologers showed up to find a two- or three-year-old Jesus in his home in Bethlehem. They gave him gifts, honoring his birth, and—here is why we call these fellas "wise men"—they identified the toddler in Bethlehem, not Herod, as the true king. For them, the hope for the people of Israel, and all humanity, was not in a palace and did not have an army.

God warned Joseph in a dream of Herod's plan to kill Jesus, so the family went into hiding in Egypt. Herod, in Pharaoh-esque fashion, slaughtered many children in hopes of eliminating Jesus—like I said, watch for the strong parallels to Moses. When Herod died and the family returned to Israel, they were told to move to Nazareth. From there, the story goes dark for a couple decades and picks back up with the ministry of John the Baptist and Jesus as a thirtysomething.

I am just glad you didn't add some visit to a guru in India to Jesus' story.

THE ELDER

Jesus' most famous sermon, the Sermon on the Mount, comes toward the beginning of Matthew. There, with his disciples gathered round him, not unlike Moses on Mount Sinai, Jesus gave the first of five discourses about the life his followers are to live. These five teachings of Jesus, combined with the story of Jesus the author borrowed from Mark, show us how Matthew understood Jesus. The teachings of Jesus are like the Torah of Moses, and those who are wise will recognize them as authoritative if they build their lives upon them. And in the end, Jesus' life and death liberate the people from (spiritual) captivity, just as Moses rescued Israel from slavery in Egypt. If Matthew

saw Jesus through a thoroughly Jewish frame, then Luke
is the evangelist who tells the Jesus story for the widest
audience.

Luke

The author of Luke is also the author of the book of Acts.
These two books are like the first and second part of the
greatest summer blockbuster franchise of all time. Taken
together, they tell the story of the Spirit of God coming
into the world in greater and greater intensity. From Mary
to Jesus, from the preaching of Peter to the evangelism of
Paul, the good news of God's kingdom is revealed in the
two-book narrative. The Gospel of Luke shares many of
the same sources as Matthew, but the social context is much
different, originating from a community of gentile (that
is, non-Jewish) converts. This is crucial to understanding Luke, and it's clear from the beginning. In contrast to
Matthew's genealogy, which works its way through David
back to Abraham, Luke's goes all the way back to Adam,
the first human and son of God. This expansion of Jesus'
lineage follows the expansive movement of the Spirit in
Luke-Acts. God's lineage with humanity predates Abraham, the father of the Hebrews, going all the way back to
Adam, the father of all humanity.

When you read the birth story in Luke, you'll find
the Christmas pageant material: the census, the donkey,
the manger, the shepherds, and the angels. But when
these specific narrative elements are set in their historical
context—namely, the Roman domination of Israel—they
become poignant indicators of what Luke is trying to do.
Like Atia, mother of Caesar Augustus, who conceived her

son through a visitation by Apollo, Mary also conceived her son from a God, but Mary is set apart because she's a virgin. Just as Caesar was called savior, lord, and son of God, Jesus was, too—but God sent angels to announce it. And unlike Caesar, Jesus was born to an unwed mother without a bed of her own, and the celebration of his birth began with those on the fringe of civilized society, shepherds.

Historical parallels like these can really help the ideas come alive in a sermon. Of course, you

THE BISHOP

might want to mention this during Advent and not when the church is full of first-time visitors.

It's almost as if Luke wanted to make sure that we see Jesus and his kingdom mission in sharp contrast to Caesar and Rome, so he invented an empire-wide tax registry. We know this never happened because Rome had quality accountants who kept detailed records, and there's no record of this census. But if you wanted to have Caesar himself give an order that forced Mary and Joseph to travel from Nazareth to Bethlehem and give birth to their son in King David's hometown, also conveniently fulfilling the messianic prophecy, then this is the perfect narrative invention. As my preaching professor used to say, "Never let the truth get in the way of a good story, especially when it's true."

In Luke-Acts, the Spirit of God is almost as central a character as Jesus. The story begins with the famous account of Mary choosing to partner with God in the conception and birth of the Messiah and being filled with the Spirit. This same Spirit was at work in the conception of

THE DEACON

In college, I worked part time at a church that was so conservative they didn't say "virgin" Mary. It was too suggestive.

Jesus' cousin John the Baptist and in old Simeon, who praised God in the temple when he saw the baby Jesus.

Mary's song, called the Magnificat, describes her joy to be the mother of the one through whom God will establish a more just social order: "He has shown strength with his arm; he has scattered the proud and the thoughts of their hearts. He has brought down the powerful from their thrones, and lifted up the lowly; he has filled the hungry with good things, and sent the rich away empty."[8] In Luke, the Spirit appears again at Jesus' baptism, and it is with the Spirit that Jesus sends out his disciples—not once as in Mark and Matthew, but twice—to proclaim and enact the kingdom of God. Then, from the cross, Jesus cries out to God saying, "Into your hands I commend my spirit," and after the resurrection he tells his disciples to wait until God sends the Spirit to them at Pentecost.[9]

In other words, the Spirit drips off of almost every page of Luke, and it's no more important than in Jesus' inaugural sermon, just after his baptism. In his hometown synagogue, Jesus stood to read from the prophet Isaiah and said, "The spirit of the Lord is upon me, because God has anointed me to bring good news to the poor, and has sent me to proclaim release to the captives and recovery of sight to the blind, to let the oppressed go free, to proclaim the year of the Lord's favor."[10] Jesus obviously shares his mom's prophetic impulse, and, what's even better, he has no problem editing out one phrase from the text he was reading: "and the day of vengeance of our God."[11]

Jesus inherits his tradition, edits out the violence, and expands it. After reading the scroll, he tells his neighbors

---

If Jesus loved his tradition enough to cut out violence and expand it to more people, shouldn't we do the same with Christianity?

THE ACOLYTE

---

that the text is being fulfilled in their hearing. This causes them to lose it—they think he's so crazy that they try to run him off a cliff. But just because Jesus loses his home-town audience doesn't mean he turns down the prophetic heat. He proceeds to remind them that both Elijah and Elisha gave special attention to gentiles who were in need. Luke is reminding his readers that the Spirit expands the blessing of the kingdom beyond the people of Israel. Luke knows that reality personally because his community was full of them.

Luke is the last of the three synoptic Gospels. As we turn to the Gospel of John, we leave behind the outline of Mark, the teachings from Q, and the concerns about Jesus' birth. In fact the only miracle carried over into John is the feeding of the five thousand. This doesn't mean John was out of the loop, but it does highlight just how unique the voice of the fourth Gospel is.

John

The Gospel of John is the most distinct of the four. For our purposes, John is the clearest about who Jesus is—after all, he explains it right there in the prologue: Jesus is the Word made flesh. All four Gospels retell the beginning of Jesus in light of his post-Easter identity—for Mark it's at his baptism, for Matthew and Luke it's his conception, and in John it goes back all the way to the literal beginning, the beginning of the creation of the cosmos.

John was appropriating two different uses of the concept of the "Word" (*Logos* in Greek) when he applied it to Christ. One came from the Hebrew Scriptures in which the "Word of God" was understood as both speech and source. In Genesis, God speaks, and this Word is the very means by which God creates the heavens and the earth. This same Word is also identified as the source of the Torah and later personified as Wisdom herself in the book of Proverbs.

The other use of Logos was from the Stoics, a school of Greek philosophy. For them the Word is an activity and a principle—to be exact, the principle of reason that runs through all the world. To know the Word and to live accordingly was the Stoic ideal. Most New Testament scholars see John appropriating both of these uses to describe Jesus as coming from the source of all and being the embodiment of God's speech and principles. It's as if, in light of the resurrection and the continued presence of God in the Christian community, they came to realize that in Christ, the source of all existence, life and light became dazzlingly clear. The God no one has seen was definitively revealed here in the Son.

This cosmic picture in the prologue of John must be ever-present in our minds throughout our encounter with this Gospel. After the prologue, the Gospel turns to the familiar baptism scene that kicks off Jesus' public ministry, but, in doing so, John is more a theologian than a journalist. The contrast between John and the Synoptics isn't hard to notice. His text doesn't share the storyline of a one-year ministry in Galilee that was established in Mark, instead describing a three-year ministry in Judea. John is also full of miracles that aren't in the other Gospels, and it doesn't contain a single parable.

Unlike in the Synoptics, in the Fourth Gospel Jesus proclaims the good news about his own coming rather than the kingdom in sayings like, "If God were your Father, you would love me, for I came from God and now I am here."[12] And in the "I Am" sayings, Jesus makes the strongest claims about his divine identity in any of the Gospels: I am the bread of life, light of the world, gate, good shepherd, resurrection, "the way, the truth, and the life," and the true vine. The contrasts between John and the other Gospels extend even to the passion week narrative. In John, Jesus is not tormented in the Garden of Gethsemane, praying for God to remove the cup of his suffering, but he is completely aware and in charge of the

THE BISHOP

I often tell my evangelical friends that using the "I Am" sayings as theological clubs just points to their biblical naiveté.

entire process. And when the soldiers come to arrest him, Jesus says, "I am he," and they fall to the ground.[13]

One could be tempted to ignore the Gospel of John altogether because, short of Jesus crying at the death of his dear friend Lazarus, there's just not much humanity in John's Jesus. For a period of my life, I wished John had been left out of the Bible, if for no other reason than how obnoxious Christians can be when putting John 3:16 on everything and using "the way, the truth, and the life" passage to threaten their neighbors and friends with hell. Here's the thing: if we just pay attention to John and listen to his testimony on his own terms, then the Gospel is pretty awesome. How beautiful is it that the same creative, divine activity that brought the world into being also shared in our material existence, developed deep friendships, and cried at the loss of one of those friends? Even more amazing is John's witness that God, who made the entire world, loves it and came not to condemn it but to redeem it (that's John 3:17).

When John's Gospel is read on its own terms, as a theological narrative uncovering the cosmic depth discovered in the life of Jesus, both the Gospel and Jesus become way cooler. If you don't believe me, then just consider Jesus' first miraculous sign in the Gospel. Jesus is at

Why don't we see that
sign held up in the stands
at sporting events?

THE DEACON

a weeklong wedding party when the wine runs out. His mom strong-arms him into fixing the problem in order to keep the party going. Jesus tries to protest, arguing that it's not time for him to kick off his ministry, but Mom prevails. Jesus turns more than a hundred gallons of water in purification jugs into the best wine around. John says that, in this act, Jesus revealed his glory, and he did so by turning water for a religious ritual into fuel for a party. That is a word from the Word that is seriously good news. I'm telling you, Jesus partied.

A Title in Search of Its Meaning

Looking at the christological testimonies in each of the Gospels reveals the genuine diversity of their accounts and conclusions. When you consider the other New Testament books, the diversity is even greater. In light of the internal skeptic of the postmodern disciple and the new variety of contemporary testimonies finally being given voice in the church, that diversity is more important today than ever before.

The Gospels don't address many of our modern theological questions directly. They can't. They are just as much a part of their historical situation as we are of ours. They do, however, give testimony to the presence of Christ in their own communities and invite us to listen and do the same today. Seeing that the story of Jesus was told differently in different communities can be freeing for us as present-day disciples, often unsure of what we can believe.

The Gospels share in common the confession that Jesus is the Christ. Beyond that, we should be careful not to impose later creeds or the will of early councils of the church on them. We have to let the Gospels be themselves. When we do, we gain multiple advantages.

For one, the perspectives they represent are the product of the church's ongoing relationship with God through the risen Christ, and that's the reality they are witnessing to. Second, the historical Jesus is not the object of faith, God is. What God was doing in the person of Jesus is the subject matter of the Gospels. Third, though the historical Jesus is not the object of faith, he can enliven and chasten our own image of the Christ. Fourth, there is more theological diversity in the four Gospels than many churches are comfortable with. They'd like to be a bit more like Tatian, but just a reminder: that's heresy!

Fifth, the gospel is not an idea, but rather a happening, an event, and the Christ event cannot be captured in a text or isolated in any one telling. It's not a truth you learn, but one you encounter. Like a meteor crashing into a giant lake, there will be waves and ripples aplenty in its wake, but they are not the meteor itself. Finally, the Gospels repeatedly present the disciples as identifying Jesus correctly while completely misunderstanding his role as the Christ.

By focusing on the variety of New Testament Christologies, we also get a model for embracing the diverse expressions of situations and cultures we're unfamiliar with. Like the early church, which saw an influx of gentiles, the destruction of the temple, geographic expansion, and a constantly developing theology, the contemporary church is also experiencing an explosion of new communities and theologies. There are more voices and cultures within the church now than ever before. Women are finally being given the dignity to share their experience of the living Christ, and there's a multiplicity of christological testimonies coming from cultures and peoples outside the West.

Yes, the biblical mandate is to transcend our present boundaries and include more and

THE BISHOP

more voices. The trick is getting the old voices soft enough they start to listen.

Those of us in the West are tempted to imagine that our ideas about Christ—our creeds, traditions, and conclusions—are not just ours but are universal, for all Christians. We're totally down with describing a homeless first-century Jew as the eternal Logos of Platonic philosophy, but when an African theologian calls Jesus her ancestor, it freaks us out. Given the sheer growth and vitality of Christianity in the global South, to ignore or dismiss these newly acknowledged voices is a whole new kind of heresy.

Reflecting on this temptation, we can look to Jesus and his encounter with the Canaanite woman in Matthew's Gospel as a model for expanding the table of theological participants. What makes Matthew's story so powerful is that his Gospel comes to us from a community that's wrestling with a giant ethnic shift toward a gentile-dominated church. As the contemporary church shifts its center to the global South, we too will have to come to grips with a changing identity.

Matthew has Jesus encounter a Canaanite woman in need of help for her daughter. The Canaanites were among the occupants of the Promised Land when Israel returned from the exodus. In the book of Joshua, the Canaanites were not greeted as possible neighbors but instead were violently demolished. At the time of Jesus, there were no more Canaanites, but their role in the history of Israel was well-known. In other words, that Matthew was telling us this story to make a very serious theological point.

> Jesus left that place and went away to the district of Tyre and Sidon. Just then a Canaanite woman from that region came out and started shouting, "Have mercy on me, Lord, Son of David; my daughter is tormented by a demon." But he did not answer her at all. And his disciples came and urged him, saying, "Send her away, for she keeps shouting after us." He answered, "I was sent only to the lost sheep of the house of Israel." But she came and knelt before him, saying, "Lord, help me." He answered, "It is not fair to take the children's food and throw it to the dogs." She said, "Yes, Lord, yet even the dogs eat the crumbs that fall from their masters' table." Then Jesus answered her, "Woman, great is your faith! Let it be done for you as you wish." And her daughter was healed instantly.[14]

This is obviously not Jesus' most amazing moment. But if even Jesus had a hard time imagining God's mission extending beyond the boundaries of his community, then perhaps we too might have the same problem. The Canaanite woman insisted that the kin-dom table even had crumbs for the dogs, and this plea cracked open the boundaries Jesus inherited. He responded by lifting her up as an example of great faith.

What better text could we use to reflect on the growing diversity of voices in the church today? Jesus gives us a way of letting the kin-dom of God be expanded and trans-

---

I can't decide if I like the idea of Jesus needing to grow into being more Christ-like. I guess I always thought of him as the means and not the model.

THE ACOLYTE

---

formed by those we see as outsiders, even those who might have formerly been conquered. This particular insight is one that Matthew can give us when his Gospel is read on its own terms and from its own situation. As we let the Gospels speak for themselves in all their diversity, we can let the divergent testimonies in our own congregations be

---

Learning to hold multiplicity with charity is something all Christians should endeavor toward in the twenty-first century.

THE ELDER

---

welcomed and thus celebrate the explosion of newness across the church. We can let the Gospels reveal to us the good news of the gospel.

5

Anselm, Luther, and the Cootie Collector

I have a confession to make: I used to be a Calvinist. For some, that label means absolutely nothing. For others, it provokes an intense response—Calvinism tends to have that effect. Where I went to college, at a small Baptist school in the South, whether you were a Calvinist really mattered, for it determined which of the fifteen campus Bible studies you could attend. By the prevenient grace of God, I was eventually lured beyond the imaginative cage of John Calvin, and I finally moved out of the Baptist enclave that rivaled Geneva for its lack of theological imagination.[1]

In a Bible Belt bubble, the spectrum of thought was rather limited, so particular questions were real dividing lines. Was the earth created in seven days of twenty-four hours each? Was God really predestining little babies to

THE DEACON

In the late 90s, my youth pastor literally had a belt that was studded with the letters "BIBLE" on it. He was also a big Five Iron Frenzy fan.

eternal conscious torment? I don't mean to imply that the nuances in these questions are entirely unimportant, it's just that to debate them requires a common framework that many lack.

Up to this point, I've tried to give you a small taste of a few things: the craziness of Christian claims about Jesus, the historians' version of the Jewish Jesus, a description of Jesus' view of the kingdom, and the content of the Gospel stories. At the heart of this book is the claim that, as Christians, *our experience and account of God is inseparable from the life and continued presence of Jesus.* Christology is a communal reality in search of an explanation. As such, the accounts are quite contextual. After the church came to dominate the West and became a virtual religious monopoly, the conversation around Christ changed.

Just how Christendom affected theology will be clear as we look at two of the most creative thinkers from the epoch of Christian dominance: Anselm of Canterbury (1033–1109) and Martin Luther (1483–1546). I'm not going to tell you everything these two guys thought about Jesus, and I'll try to avoid criticizing them from my own twenty-first-century point of view. What I hope to do is describe how Anselm and Luther gave voice to the experience of God as mediated by Jesus in their eras, through their own particular cultural lenses. As I try to make these older accounts of Jesus have some zing, perhaps we can start to see them as members in a long line of Christ-confessors and not place expectations on their proclamations that they can't handle.

We've Got the Answer, So What's the Question?

I have another confession to make. I hate blood talk, especially when it comes to Jesus. If a minister gets all worked up about Jesus' blood washing away sin, or we sing a hymn with the line, "There is a fountain filled with blood, drawn from Immanuel's veins," I get a bit sick to my stomach—and it's not the Holy Spirit convicting me, either. For me, there's nothing exciting, liberating, or inspirational about Jesus' blood. I do not believe that God needed blood to forgive me. In fact, the idea that there's a dichotomy within the character of Godself—that the Father was out for the blood of the Son in order to forgive humanity—is entirely ludicrous. You would think that Jesus' being the "image of the invisible God" would clear things up and not muddy—or bloody—the water.

Remember when Mel Gibson's *The Passion of the Christ* came out? As a religion major who had an opinion about everything, I joined a group of friends and went to see the movie. After a couple hours of watching Jesus' constant torture, almost everyone was relieved when the film ended. We proceeded to a local coffee shop, and that's when the talking began. My favorite parts of the film were the flashbacks to Jesus' ministry (especially the part where

THE DEACON

My church rented out an entire theater at the local cineplex, and we handed out tracts to all the heathens seeing *Kill Bill: Volume 2.*

we learn that he invented the upright chair and table). While some of my friends focused on the running battle between Jesus and Satan, most were moved by the sheer beating Jesus took on their behalf. Each crack and pull of the whip, tearing flesh from Jesus' back, was punishment that *he* endured *for them*. It was overpowering and unnerving to see God's wrath poured out on the big screen like that.

Underneath our responses were different questions that we each brought to the film. We knew that Jesus was the *answer*, but each of us came with our own *questions*. Some of those questions had to do with the way that we are "saved" by Jesus. Theologians call the various answers to these questions doctrines of atonement.

THE ACOLYTE

I assume this is unrelated to the movie by the same name. At least I hope so.

Atonement is just the sweet vocab word for what God did in Christ on the cross that we could not do for ourselves. It's how we describe God's gift to us. This is important because some people love arguing about the mechanism of God's action itself, insisting that their particular description is the correct, biblical account. But here's the thing: there isn't just one biblical account—there are many! I'll prove that to you by the end of this chapter, but we'll start with a medieval dude who launched the version of the atonement that most of us heard at church camp.

Anselm: Why the God-Man?

The single most influential Christology after Paul's is that of Anselm of Canterbury, an eleventh-century Benedictine monk. To this day, introduction to philosophy classes tackle his ontological proof for the existence of God, and there's hardly a more foundational text in Christology than *Cur Deus Homo* (*Why a God-Man?*).

I don't get arguing for the existence of God. It's always either a pat on the back or another annoying Christian feeling smart.

THE ELDER

Despite his notoriety, Anselm is a contentious figure among nerds who have strong opinions about medieval theologians. I'm sure all the people emotionally invested in assessing medieval theology could fit on one (small) cruise ship, yet Anselm's view of the atonement, often labeled the *satisfaction theory*, continues to provoke important discussions concerning power and privilege in theology. Let's start by looking at exactly what he said.

Anselm was frustrated with the dominant atonement theory in his day, which said that between the crucifixion and resurrection, Jesus went down to hell and beat the snot out of Satan, thereby freeing humanity from satanic captivity. Anselm had major issues with the starring role given the devil. He thought it ridiculous that God came in Christ to deal solely with the Evil One. As a philosopher, Anselm was skeptical that the words about Satan in the Bible were to be taken literally. And he was confident that

THE BISHOP

I would like to second Anselm's rejection of the pitchforked Evil One.

fixating on the devil was detrimental to the church. So, if God did not become incarnate to ransom humanity back from the devil, then why the God-man?

What drove Anselm was a desire to make sense of the incarnation—that God came to earth in human form. He was a logical guy, so he assumed that there was a rational necessity for the incarnation, and this necessity was his starting point. Human beings were created by God as rational creatures, made to find their happiness through obedience to God's will, and humanity's ultimate happiness is eternal life with God. Sin and human disobedience, he argued, is a blockage between God and humanity, rendering impossible God's true desires for humanity.

Now, Anselm assumed a few things. First, for Anselm, God created humanity to share in the divine life.

Being rational creatures and bearing the divine image, we were made to participate in God's eternal life. It's just that the very things that make it possible for us to share in God's divine life create the predicament of sin. Second, God would not be deterred by sin but would instead seek to overcome it. Sin is our problem in one sense, but it's also God's problem. In fact, since we can't overcome it, it's more a problem for the God who loves us than ours.

If sin is more God's problem than ours, then why create things this way?

THE ACOLYTE

In his attempt to give voice to the predicament of sin in his day, Anselm turned to the honor system within feudal society, where there was a relationship between the proper honor one was due and one's place in the social hierarchy. Justice was understood as giving what was due, and, in the case of an infraction, justice required paying what was owed. This dynamic went both ways in a feudal society. A serf owed less honor to his peer than to his lord. Likewise, the responsibility of the lord was greater, given his charge over the land and its people.

When Anselm transposed this arrangement to the infinite God and the finite creation, he found the question that has a God-man as the answer. Here's how that works: the infinite God of all creation is superior in every way to a finite ruler. Thus, sin puts humanity in an infinite debt. The elimination of this debt comes by rendering what is due, and this is what Anselm calls *satisfaction*. The problem for humanity is that the magnitude of our dishonor is infinite but we are finite. Even worse, since all humanity is born into the sin of Adam, even a perfectly obedient human could not make satisfaction; a perfectly obedient life would simply be what was due to God *before* humanity's fall; the debt of the original sinners, Adam and Eve would still be owed. It's the magnitude of God's honor that creates an asymmetry between God and humanity and necessitates the incarnation of the God-man. For Anselm, it's the responsibility of *God* for God's land and God's people that requires the incarnation and the crucifixion.

In the development of this vision, Anselm put forward two strong questions that he assumes his intelligent readers are asking. First, *why can't God send a mediating figure between God and humanity instead of the God-man?* To this, Anselm says that a mediating figure may have been able to do *some* good, but since God wants to share the divine life with humanity, the honor of God must be completely satisfied. (P.S. This means God doesn't want to just make nice, but embrace all of us.)

And second, *why can't God just freely give mercy to humanity?* It seems like God is jumping through a bunch of hoops to extend mercy, and that doesn't seem very Godlike. Well, Anselm countered, God cannot have an act of will where one attribute is set against another, so God's divine simplicity requires the act of satisfaction to be congruent with God's entire nature. If God desires satisfaction, the payment must come from humanity. And if only God can satisfy such a debt, then the God-man is necessary.

In previous versions of the atonement, the suffering and sacrifice of Christ brought about the reconciliation between God and humans. But for Anselm, God did not demand suffering for the remission of sin or to free humanity from the devil. Humanity owed God an infinite debt that could only be satisfied through the God-man.

Differentiating owing a debt and God's desire for suffering would have made youth group less painful.

THE DEACON

Two features of Christ's obedience made that satisfaction possible. First, the human person of Jesus was obedient to God throughout his life, which means that, as a human, he gave God what was due. (Here, the full faithfulness of Jesus, not his sinlessness, is emphasized.) With that obedient life, Jesus of Nazareth paid his own way to eternal life, but there was still that pesky inheritance from Adam to deal with. So, second, Christ as God gave *more* than was owed through his obedience. The Son was "obedient to death on a cross," as Paul wrote; he was not forced by the Father.[2] When obedience is understood—as

---

The obedience of Christ also became a central theme for Anselm's devotion, along with the obedience of Mary.

THE DEACON

Anselm understands it—as having a will congruent to that of God, it is the Son's obedient choice that pleased the Father, not necessarily the act of suffering itself. The Son, who was obedient to death, is honored by God. But the Son does not need the reward himself, so he, in another act of obedience, shares it with the objects of God's love—humanity. In Anselm's mind, the God-man alone can make satisfaction for us by paying the debt we owe God.

When Anselm made this argument in *Cur Deus Homo*, it was a medieval best-seller—they were pumping out copies as fast as the monks would write them, which wasn't very fast. But the point is, Anselm's theory of the atonement captured everyone's attention in Europe because it accorded almost perfectly with their own experience of life. The fact that it still holds on today, long after the feudal system has died, is less understandable.

The feudal system politically gave way to the rise of nation states. Religiously, this was the beginning of the Reformation. What the most prominent reformer, Martin Luther, was responding to was the perversion of Anselm's vision. Imagine that as time goes by access to the surplus of satisfaction the God-Man brought was monetized, not to feed the hungry, but to line the coffers of Rome. That's where Luther shows up.

Luther: What Must I Do to Be Saved?

In the sixteenth century, the church experienced its biggest upheaval, what we call the Reformation. At its center was Martin Luther, a nerdy Augustinian monk who loved beer and turned the monasteries he emptied into hybrid seminaries with in-house breweries.[3] He was also

That's a seriously
awesome footnote.

THE DEACON

bedeviled by despair. Luther suffered from anxiety about
the judgment of God, which he felt as a daily, palpable
threat. As the story goes, lightning struck the ground near
him while he was riding a horse home one day. In sheer
terror, he cried out for divine protection and professed, "I
will become a monk!" He rode the rest of the way home
and told his father, who was hoping he'd be a lawyer,
about his vow.

Promises were important to Luther and sat at the
very heart of his understanding of the gospel. As a dutiful monk, he was plagued by guilt, confessing his sins with
a frequency and intensity that his confessor (who listened
every day to a bunch of dudes so into Jesus they were celi-
bate) had never seen. The church had become rather creative in using guilt and God's wrath as a motivational tool
for fund-raising. They took the economy of divine mercy
and monetized it—just like the blog you used to read all the
time but no longer visit because it's now behind a paywall.

What is a blog, and how
can I build a paywall
around my church?

THE ELDER

Luther was hardcore. He put tons of energy into
being the perfect monk without realizing that he might

THE DEACON

He was the "Most Interesting Theologian in the World." Sin boldly, my friends.

be doing it wrong. The idea that God may indeed love him and want him to live free from guilt, shame, fear, and anxiety didn't cross his mind. He was more concerned with managing his guilt and God's wrath.

The breakthrough for Luther came in the confession booth. In the very space where time after time he brought his beleaguered conscience, confessed his sins, and received the priest's absolution, Luther had an epiphany: he heard the words of forgiveness not as the obligatory response from a well-meaning confessor, but as the very words of Christ. Christ himself offered Luther forgiveness, just as Christ himself promised to be present in the Eucharist. This was good news to Luther: he was forgiven, and he was justified by faith alone. After all, when Christ tells you that your sins are forgiven, who are you to think of yourself as *just* a sinner?

Luther was in search of genuine freedom, and, for him, the freedom of the Christian was inconceivable unless the law gave us an awareness of our bondage to sin. As long as you believe that you can save yourself, then you're not able to experience the fullness of the gospel. The law demonstrates that you can do nothing good on your own, and, believe it or not, this is really good news: since you can't actually do anything good, you don't have to. The gospel, for Luther, is the promise of grace from God in Christ. The promise of God is not a reward for doing something—it's the gift of Christ. And you, a sinner, are justified by faith alone, apart from your actions. What Luther emphasized was the "for me" aspect of the gospel. The Christian does not simply have faith that Jesus was incarnate, was born of Mary, died, and rose again, but has faith that this good news is *for us, personally, each one of us.*

I love Luther's personal imagery, but I'm always reminded that many parishioners don't prefer such personal images of God.

THE BISHOP

To explain this, Luther used the image of wedding vows, which he termed the "blessed exchange." In this parable, the believer was likened to a harlot who came to marry the son of the king. Through the marriage vows, the bridegroom (hint: Christ) promised to receive all of his beloved's sin and debts while giving the bride all the good stuff. The bride did nothing, contributed nothing, but gained all the wealth and status of the groom. By simply trusting the vows of her groom, the bride would receive royal status and would be subject to none. In Christ, God says to each one of us, "What's mine is yours and what's yours is mine, for you are my beloved." When the one who speaks these words is the God who made you, knows you completely, and loves you completely, there are no truer words.

Personally, I've never bought into Luther's despair because I've never believed that God is that angry at me. I assume that if God is anything like Jesus, then living in fear is a waste of time. But a few things Luther said remain wonderfully insightful.

THE DEACON

Exactly! I've heard Tripp say: "God should at least be as nice as Jesus."

Luther was a realist about human beings. He knew that we are pretty screwed up—he'd never buy the myth of freedom in our modern age. We assume that we are free. We imagine that with the proper knowledge and solid reasoning we can do the right thing, and when we don't, we ought to be held responsible for our poor choices. That's nuts, and Luther knew it. The problem isn't our decision making or the particular sins we commit. The problem is sin itself—our entire state of being. For Luther, sin was about our spiritual enslavement, which runs to the very core of our being and not any particular action. While this may ruin our image of human exceptionalism, it's really good news, for it frees us from having to be the answer to our own problem. That's a serious relief.

Also, when we recognize that each of us is simultaneously saint and sinner—a major theme for Luther—we can be a bit more gracious with each other and with ourselves. Being aware that the human predicament involves doing horrible things we don't want to do and not doing good things we intend to do can be freeing. We shouldn't reliquish our desire for personal maturity and a more beautiful world, but we can also celebrate smaller victories and be ready to offer forgiveness to each other along the way.

"You may think you suck, but God thinks you are bad ass" should be the motto of every middle-school youth ministry.

THE ACOLYTE

Luther's description of grace remains helpful even though I don't dread God's judgment. It doesn't take an angry heavenly Father for us to believe lies about ourselves. We all have things we believe about ourselves that stack up in our souls: "You aren't good enough." "What a waste." "If they only knew, they wouldn't love you." According to Luther, those words are straight-up lies. They are not true about you, me, or the person you said them to. We can say them to ourselves, our kids, our friends, or our coworkers with biting precision, but they just aren't true. Why not? Because the God who made the entire world knows your name and cares about you. God has the truest word about you: "You are God's beloved." You didn't earn it, you don't deserve it, but God believes you're worth it.

The crazy thing about this understanding of the gospel is that it calls us to be more ethical and more responsible than a vision of reality where we are stuck trying to sing for our supper does. We do not *have* to do good works, we *get* to. Living a life for beauty and justice can occur from a place of abundance and not judgment, in a community of cheer and not shame. The gospel is not a technique for getting saved, and it's definitely not practical advice about how to live our lives. It's way too good and way too practical for that. The gospel changes us from the inside out. And Jesus is the key, for he bridged humanity and divinity.

Did You Have Cooties Too?

Sometimes the simple act of answering a question is a problem. Not all questions are created equal, for they come wrapped up in all kinds of assumptions. For example, where did cooties come from? That's one my five-year-old son asked me, and I was totally unprepared for it. I took the bait. I answered.

Before telling you about my parental failure when dealing with the cooties question, I should quickly explain cooties to you. If it's been a while since you interacted with a preschooler dealing with a cootie break-out, you may think I am talking about the insect cousin of head lice or bedbugs. Nope. As that most esteemed collection of crowdsourced scholarly definitions, the *Urban Dictionary*, puts it, cooties can be defined as the following:

1. Highly contagious, viral bacteria that breed inside young females and are released into the air via sweat glands when in the proximity of young boys.

I do hope you didn't show your five-year-old Urban Dictionary. BTW, it's NSFW.

THE BISHOP

2. Imaginary infestations of the truly un-cool.
3. A disease that only girls have! Boys cannot get it because of their awesomeness!
4. Cooties are an imaginary affliction from childhood transferable by touch. It's a way of little girls telling other little girls not to play with boys and vice versa.[4]

Such clarity. Clearly no theologian was involved in the creation of such precise definitions.

One day we were driving home from my son's preschool when he explained that there was a case of the cooties running rampant through his class. Luckily, they discovered a way to limit the damage by designating the kid who would have cooties for the day and then rotating to another kid after just one day of being ostracized.[5]

"Did you and Mom have cooties when you were in preschool?" he asked.

"Of course we did. Don't worry, everyone grows out of them."

"Do you have to touch someone's nose to share it?"

"Oh no, I am pretty sure it's transferable through any nonviolent, playground-appropriate contact. You definitely don't need to be touching noses unless you are helping a buddy pick their nose."

"No, Dad, that's gross. But if your friend has cooties, can you help them? You know, can you get rid of the cooties so we can play Star Wars on the playground again?"

I wanted so badly to take back everything I had said up to that point and say, "There are *no* cooties," but I'd already bitten the bullet. And so I did what every father does in that situation, I joined the mythological game and created an imaginary cure for the imaginary affliction: I told Elgin about magic pretzel sticks. They look and taste just like regular ones. In fact, no one can tell the difference between them and plain old pretzel sticks except that if you eat a magic pretzel stick, you can no longer get cooties. You will be permanently inoculated against them. If you give one to your best friend, he will be cootie-free and you can resume being Han Solo and Chewbacca on the playground. Obviously, parents traditionally save these magic pretzel sticks for the end of preschool as a vaccination prior to beginning kindergarten, but sharing them early seemed appropriate under the circumstances.

You see, I was stuck. In deciding to answer a really bad question, I gave cooties power. Then I proceeded to add magic to myth with pretzel sticks. My intentions were good, for I'm pretty confident that playing Star Wars on

THE DEACON

Did God also invent fatherhood so they can purchase Star Wars Lego as gifts for their kids?

the playground is one of reasons God gave for creating five-year-old boys. The idea that two friends wouldn't be playing together because of cooties would irk any parent. None of us would want our kids to miss the thrill of imaginative play for an imaginary reason.

Here's the problem: it doesn't matter if cooties are real or not. If they define the terms of engagement on the playground, then they're real. They are made real by those under the threat of contagion. Cooties are given the power to separate people, evaluate people, shun people, and create barriers to enjoying all that playground life has to offer. The predicament of cooties is very real when you're on the playground. The sad thing is that we never really outgrow them.

We all have cooties. We know, depending on the playground, just which parts of us are to be kept under wraps, which secrets have to stay hidden, which questions can't be asked, and which struggles we can't share.

We know who has cooties. We know who to avoid, who to ignore, when to leave, and how to avoid being attached to *them*. One of the sick and twisted parts of being human is how tribal we are and how natural it is to define ourselves and our community over against others. When we leave the literal playground behind, we manage to keep the metaphorical playground alive in our families, churches, careers, politics, and anyplace we let an imaginary affliction reign over us.

Cooties are real. Sometimes cooties are about who you are, about what makes you different than the rest of those on the playground. Sometimes cooties are about guilt, about the things you have done that, should they become known, mark you and send you off to the corner of the yard to spend recess alone. Sometimes cooties are about shame, about burdens you carry that are not of your own making. Shame can be the result of what has happened to you, as in the case of abuse, or it can be the result of the guilt you feel from locking those particular elements of your history in a dark closet.

I remember the first time I dared to tell someone about the shame I carried. I had carried the burden for years, lost many nights of sleep, and tried to overcompensate for it by being the most awesome son, brother, friend, student, and Christian ever. Back then, I couldn't distinguish between guilt and shame, and I'd thought God was critiquing me for what had happened. Then, I risked a moment of honesty with a trusted mentor, and I discovered that I was still lovable. With everything on the table, I was affirmed as if for the first time. I heard the words, "Tripp, you are a new creation in Christ," as if I were Lazarus walking out of the tomb, because this time those words were not about the Tripp I let out during the day when people were watching, but about the one I went to sleep with each night.

When I was freed from the shame and I realized that there were no cooties, my existence was renewed and deepened.

Jesus was God's cootie collector. Throughout his ministry, he collected cooties from every playground across Israel, all the while proclaiming that they didn't even exist. He managed to pick them up from lepers, prostitutes, drunkards, Pharisees, the demonically possessed, Roman centurions, rich tax collectors, Zealots, John the Baptist, kids, the rich women funding his ministry, and his ragtag collection of disciples. All in all, he managed to disturb so many different playgrounds that they all conspired to kill him, to put him to death and further instantiate the reality of cooties.

But the yes of the world, terrorized yet protecting its own infection, was not the last word. God had the last word and said no. Through the resurrection of Christ, the cootie collector made a comeback, saying loud and proud that there were and there definitely still are *no cooties.*

This is, in part, what we can learn from the christological efforts of both Anselm and Luther. In Anselm, we see that God has refused to be God without us. The answer to his question—why the God-man?—is us, God's creation. Anselm describes how he sees God giving us a share in the divine life through Christ. In Luther, the good news of the gospel is that the God who made us and knows us loves us completely. Through Christ, we come to hear and trust God's good word about us. Though they were articulated

---

That will preach! May
we all come to trust
God's pronouncement
over us.

THE BISHOP

---

in language and images of their own time, these powerful testimonies to God's work in Christ tell us that we live in a world where the rumors, lies, guilt, shame, and fragmented parts of our selves don't have the last word. And, if you ask me, that's a bit of good news from the eleventh and sixteenth centuries.

Getting High with Jesus

At the bottom of my first theology paper in college, the professor wrote, "This was an excellent essay. Your confusion around methodological demarcations, categorizing tools for assessment, and some ambiguity around the nature of historical thematization in terms of revelation will not permit a higher grade—but it is clear you will get there. Get a theological dictionary."

I took the paper to a couple of upperclass religion majors for a translation. I was pretty sure the sentence meant something important, but I had no idea what it was. Over the course of an hour I discovered the secret of theology nerd vocabulary, and my teacher's mysterious comment was decoded like Thorin Oakenshield's map of the Lonely Mountain in the moonlight in *The Hobbit*. In my college notebook, I wrote down the key to the christological map, and I've added to that key ever since.

THE DEACON

Okay, Nerds, it's only in the movie that Elrond explains the map to the Lonely Mountain. In the book Thorin explains Durin's Day.

My professor's comments were like an optometrist's collection of lenses, slowly bringing things into focus and giving clarity I couldn't have established any other way. The first question I wrote in my notebook was, "How can we talk about God?" Obviously, anyone can talk about *God*—after all, it's just a word. The theological question about *how* we talk about God is really whether we can have any confidence at all that there's even a smidgen of correspondence between our concept of *God* and the actual, transcendent Other. I could have asked it like this:

THE ACOLYTE

Why are there theologians who talk about "God" but don't actually believe there is a real God?

Does our language about God have any traction? What makes us think that our talk of God is connected to an actual deity and not simply a human projection? Is God just a child of our own collective making over the course of our evolutionary history? Many think so.

In order to talk about God critically as theologians do, you must use credible sources. Otherwise, what are you basing your words about God on? *Revelation* is the term we give to this type of content, and under this umbrella, theologians distinguish between *natural revelation* and *special revelation*. The former is whatever knowledge of God

---

So, when are you gonna address the thing about the four horsemen and the dragons? Since I

THE DEACON

became emergent, I still haven't made peace with that whole Revelation thing.

---

is available to us in creation, both preserved within us as image bearers of God and discoverable through the use of human reason. In Romans, Paul writes, "Ever since the creation of the world his eternal power and divine nature, invisible though they are, have been understood and seen through the things he has made. So they are without excuse."[1] He then goes on to say that humans are pretty sinful and that they have made very little use of this natural connection to God. Nevertheless, whatever aspect of God is discernible apart from specific divine action is, according to Paul, natural revelation. People like Thomas Aquinas think natural revelation is totally awesome, and others like Karl Barth are not fans at all, but they both agree that there's a difference between natural and special revelation.

Special revelation is the knowledge of God that's given in and through specific acts of God. This knowledge is not something we can discover on our own, for it must be given to us by God. Theologians argue about what counts as *special*. Is the special revelation the Bible itself? The historical acts of God recorded in the Bible? The existential encounter with God articulated by the biblical authors? Or perhaps it's God's word itself? (Of course, for that last one to hold, the definition of "God's word" would be fought over for a couple months first.) But the point remains, special revelation is when God tells us who God is. It's like the difference between you checking out my Facebook page, and you actually having a beer with me. Hearing from me directly would be *special* after all.

THE ACOLYTE

You've questioned whether God-language has any traction, so how am I supposed to pin down God speaking about herself?

One of the reasons Christology is so weird is that it's almost totally based on special revelation. You can hike to the top of a mountain, look at the stars, and have a magical moment that even Instagram can't capture—yet, even then, all you could really say is that the grandeur of creation evokes a sense of gratitude and majesty that makes you believe in a Creator.[2] But unless you have already decided that Christ is the "first born of all creation through whom all things came into being," then this image of the invisible God from Colossians would not be evoked from just one evening under the stars.[3] In other words, gawking at the stars would not naturally lead you to confess Christ. It is only *after* Jesus is identified as the person in whom God was uniquely present that you could reach such conclusions. I am not saying that the author of Colossians was right or wrong; I'm just saying that without the special revelation of God in Christ, you wouldn't find Jesus in the sunset.

The second question those upperclass students asked me was, "Where do you start when you're doing Christology?" In my paper, I confused theologians who do Christology from *below* or *above* with those who have a *low* or *high* Christology. Yes, they both seem like synonymous ideas with a common "altitude" theme, but they really do mean something different. Where a theologian starts her work does not necessarily determine where she ends it.

If your Christology is from *below*, you start with what we can know about the historical Jesus. You begin with that which we can empirically know, based on the latest research and scholarship, and you develop a theory about Jesus as the Christ from there.

Christology from below was pioneered by Wolfhart Pannenberg in his text *Jesus: God and Man*. #themoreyouknow #nerdalert

THE ELDER

But if you're coming from above, you begin with the church's christological definition as established at the ecumenical councils: Jesus was fully human and fully divine. Starting from above is simply beginning with hard-fought conclusions from the first four hundred years of the church. Here, the theologian's text will take a *descending* trajectory as it unpacks classical claims in light of our contemporary questions and challenges, especially those related to Jesus' supernatural acts.

More conservative theologians treat the Chalcedonian definition (which is a nerdy way of saying the things in the creed) as the boundary marker for doing theology— if you don't affirm the full divinity and humanity of Jesus, you may not pass Go, you may not collect $200. But they're wrong. Karl Rahner, the twentieth century's great-

---

THE BISHOP

Rahner represents the type of theological generosity the church needs more of. If only he could visit a few of my parishes.

---

est Catholic theologian, argued that the tradition should be where we *begin*, not necessarily where we end. For Rahner, a robust christological affirmation is the platform from which you jump, not the place to which all questions lead. So what's important for us to catch is that the terms *below* and *above* are merely methodological distinctions— that is, how you do your Christology.

The third question I had to answer was, "How do you assess different Christologies?" And that's when the religion majors taught me about *high* and *low*: a low

Christology is one that denies or modifies the understanding of Jesus' divinity to something less than the classical affirmation, and a high claim is that he was fully divine.

The funny thing about the use of *low* and *high* as distinctions is that you'd be hard-pressed to find a Christian theologian who'd admit to having a very low Christology. Instead, they're more likely to affirm as much as they can, given the contemporary challenges to traditional Christology. For more progressive Christian theologians, the notion of theological faithfulness is not about the repetition of particular ideas, words, or doctrines, since human language is our creature and constantly in flux. Instead, to be faithful is to attend to the energy and zeal that lies beneath the traditional verbiage.

The Raw Christological Material

We look to Scripture to ground and guide our theological constructions, but as we've already seen, the New Testament is full of different Christologies, and none of them fully accords with what was decided at Chalcedon, the last ecumenical council of the entire church in 451. Personally, I am glad it's that way. Imagine if the Bible had a giant systematic theology right in the middle. Theology would be really boring if all the answers were set out there for us, and a living faith doesn't work like that anyway. Once we realize that the act of theologizing is itself an act of testimony, then praising conformity isn't very attractive. We engage the Scriptures not as if they were a report of what happened at that time, but as a witness to the presence of the living God now.

For instance, the Bible mainly talks about Jesus in terms of how people experienced him. Sure, there's symbolic language too, but even the most conceptual language in the latest New Testament texts comes to us through the experience of the apostles.

This tension can play out two different ways, from above or from below. When we say Jesus is the "Word of God" or "Son of God," we are using symbolic language that communicates the transcendent God's revelation in Christ. In contrast, when we begin with the Spirit of God as the centering symbol for understanding Jesus, we begin from below, from God's immanent presence in the world, seeing Jesus' unity with God as coming from an intensity of what is always, already present, the Spirit.

While some of us will prefer beginning from *below* and others from *above,* what you need to remain aware of is this: each of us really begins from *within.* You may prefer starting from below for apologetic purposes, or from above for ecclesiastical reasons, but theology is not a spectator sport. Christian theology is a disciple's discipline. The very act of beginning the theological task comes after you've confessed Jesus as the Christ. This confession is neither the conclusion nor the beginning, but instead it is the very place from which you do Christology at all. If you don't confess Christ, you may be studying Christianity, but you aren't doing theology.

My First (Christological) Crush

This is a story about the first Christology I ever fell in love with: Logos Christology. (Yes, it was nerd love.)

For Christians, the Word of God is not the Bible, it's Jesus Christ. Paul calls Jesus "God's wisdom, secret and hidden, which God decreed before the ages for our glory." In Colossians, we read that Christ "is the image of the invisible God, the firstborn of all creation." And most explicitly, in John we hear of the Word made flesh.[4] This is the symbolic network of texts that inform what came to be called "Logos Christology."

Logos Christologies follow three stages. They begin in the beginning, with a preexistent Word existing even prior to God's decision to create. The second stage is the descent of the Word into the world—either in the incarnation (in John's prologue) or the crucifixion (in Philippians). The final stage is the resurrection of Jesus and his ascension to his rightful place in the divine life.

In the early church, this threefold symbol found legs and became quite popular. The early advocates of a Logos Christology, such as Justin Martyr (100–165 CE), used the symbolic imagery to answer questions beyond the text. For example, Justin sought to explain the relationship between the Word incarnate in Christ and the two wisdom traditions he was regularly engaging—Judaism and Greek philosophy. Justin insisted that anyplace and everyplace truth was found, it was both of God and from the Word. Since the Word existed with God prior to creation,

---

I am glad they don't talk about the Logos' seminal presence at my church.

THE ELDER

what became flesh in Jesus was seminally present prior to the incarnation.

Justin famously said, "They who lived with the logos are Christians, even though they have been thought atheists; as among the Greeks, Socrates and Heraclitus, and people like them; and among the barbarians, Abraham."[5] Yep, he's calling people Christians, even though they lived before Jesus. Clearly, the question that Justin was answering had to do with Christ, but it didn't exist in the first few generations of the church. His creative interpretation of the symbolic language "Word of God" allowed him to wrestle with new questions informed by his faith.

One contemporary theologian who has developed an influential Logos Christology is John Cobb. Just so you know, I love John Cobb both as a theologian and as a person. I first encountered Cobb's work in college. I had spent

---

THE DEACON

Tripp is a self-proclaimed John Cobb #FANiac, an evangelist for this JC, and even named a beer after him.

---

quite a bit of time studying the historical Jesus and the evolution of Christology in the early church. Because of this, I found the traditional explanation of Jesus' divinity problematic. Having an individual fully human and fully divine at the same time is hard enough even before you realize that the historical Jesus would have hated any such characterization. The more I came to realize the role that

Greek philosophy played in the development of the doctrine itself, the more discomfort I felt.

I ended up in a reading group on the development of Christology in the early church, and I was frustrated that smart people were taking such antiquated ideas seriously. I couldn't find much use for Christians unwilling to use historical or scientific thinking. The twenty year old version of me was extremely obnoxious about it too, and he knew more than I do now about everything under the sun (except for my own ignorance). Puffed up and insisting on an answer, I scheduled a meeting with one of my professors, and I dug in my heels. Back then, I would come to an argument with a number of ideas that I assumed the other person believed but that I found questionable. To this debate . . . er, conversation, I brought three things:

1. Knowing the historical Jesus did not see himself as the Son of God, preexistent, or divine, you ridiculously still believe that the creedal affirmations are true in a substantive sense.

2. You think that the early church fathers had a better account of Jesus' relationship to God than the authors of the Bible, and therefore you're basically willing to call Paul and Mark heretics.

3. You still believe that the hypostatic union is a doctrine that explains something other than the early church fathers' reliance on Platonic philosophy. (The hypostatic union is the church's answer to how the full divinity and humanity of Jesus can completely share the single human existence of Jesus. Yes, it's paradoxical, and yes, they invented a new word.)

My professor was extremely gracious to such a snot of a student. After explaining some of the intricacies of classical Christology, she recommended I check out *Encountering Jesus: A Debate on Christology* from the library, hinting that I would probably find John Cobb's position illuminating.[6]

She was right, I did.

The Logos, Liberally Applied

What I discovered in reading Cobb's Christology, and other Logos Christologies since, is a conversation that attempts to understand the unique, particular, and singular reality of Christ on a cosmological scale. It's pretty easy in light of contemporary science, religious pluralism, and historical scholarship to decide these big issues just can't be tackled. But, if you think of Christology from the symbol of the Logos, it's possible to affirm a robust version of the doctrine despite these aforementioned issues. Let's look at John's prologue, and then I'll sketch how Cobb develops his Christology to tackle these new theological questions.

> In the beginning was the Word, and the Word was with God, and the Word was God. He was in the beginning with God. All things came into being through him, and without him not one thing came into being. What has come into being in him was life, and the life was the light of all people. The light shines in the darkness, and the darkness did not overcome it.[7]

John Cobb's Logos Christology is an example of a Christology *from above*, in that the Logos, the eternal

Word, is incarnate in Jesus. That's the starting point. The most pressing question Cobb raises is that of religious pluralism: Can a Christian affirm that God was incarnate in Jesus *and* recognize the validity of other religious traditions? He says yes.

In addition, Cobb has a theological commitment to *naturalism*. That means Cobb's larger philosophy and understanding of God is one in which God does not act *upon* the world but instead acts within it. In other words, God does not break the laws of nature.

Cobb begins his Christology by returning to the creedal tradition, and he immediately confronts the frustrating doctrine of the hypostatic union. In the philosophy of the early first millennium, the primary building block of existence was *substance*, and a substance, by definition, cannot exist in the same place as another substance. This creates a bit of a problem if you're a theologian who knows that Jesus was a real human being and that Jesus was also God. Figuring out how these two substances, humanity and divinity, can be in the same place at the same time was essentially unsolvable. One way around this conundrum was by subtraction. For example, Jesus was fully human, except that his human will was replaced with a divine one; or, alternatively, his human mind or soul or spirit was removed and replaced with a divine version.

The church consistently affirmed the full humanity of Jesus, adding entire lines to the creeds just to make sure that none of the divinity-by-subtraction suggestions stuck. The official answer to this predicament was the *hypostatic union*, the authoritative assertion that both human and divine natures coexisted in one single *hypostasis*, or substance. This solution preserved the full humanity

THE ACOLYTE

So . . . two natures in one substance? This sounds like you may be confusing the meaning of elements.

of Jesus since nothing had to be subtracted, but Cobb is unconvinced that a new vocabulary word solves the issue. But it did confirm an orthodox Christology, at least for a few centuries. First, Jesus was as human as any of us is human, and to deny his humanity in any way is heresy. Second, God was in Christ completely, which was important because the early church recognized that God was redeeming not just human souls, but all of us in our complete embodiedness. Third, the answer to these two questions is the same:

Q: What is God like? A: Jesus.

Q: What does it mean to be fully human? A: Jesus.

When Cobb examines the church's christological debates, he finds beautiful affirmations about God in Christ that become virtually unintelligible when rendered philosophically. The incarnation of God in Jesus, which inspired the church's dogged insistence on the hypostatic union, could today be articulated with the same faith and passion, but without the substance (philosophically speaking)! Within Cobb's process theology, the paradoxical mutual indwelling of God and humanity in Jesus is actually entirely natural. Cobb is a philosophical panentheist, which means that he believes that all the world is within God, but God is more than just the world.

Cobb understands there to be two different poles in God. One he calls the *primordial nature*, which is that part of God that is constant and always the same. The other pole is called the *consequent nature*, the part of God that dwells in the world, sharing and experiencing the ongoing process of existence. In each moment, each pole has a function. The primordial nature of God discloses to the creatures their future possibilities, luring the creature to respond toward God's desired aim. And thus, the consequent nature of God takes up what has become history and redeems it as it is brought into the divine life. Knowing the world completely, inside and out, God lures the world in the next moment toward the most beautiful, true, good, adventurous, and zesty possibility.

I like to think of the process like a pizza slice. The tip of the slice is the beginning of a moment; it's where you

---

Pizza! I know about pizza. It's like kryptonite . . . it's my weakness.

THE DEACON

---

begin. From that first bite, a spectrum of possibilities is available, running the length of the slice to the crust. The reality of what we inherit in each moment eliminates most possibilities—you only have one slice to work with. While writing this paragraph, the idea of ordering pizza came into my head, and I realized it is two hours past mealtime. Theoretically I could call one in right now, I could go grab some carrot sticks to pacify the hunger, or I could just keep typing until the thought of a thin-crust pizza with pepperoni and jalapeños is the only possible decision. Each of those is a real possibility; a calorie-free pizza magically appearing before me when I wave my son's magic wand, however, is not a possibility.

In each moment there are three powers: the past, the divine lure, and creaturely freedom. God knows the past completely and desires the best for all creatures, so God persuasively acts by giving each moment an initial aim—a call toward deeper beauty. This aim is always toward the best possible outcome, but we also have a say. Whatever comes into being is then the next place God arrives, offering the grace of a new beginning. It's our decision that establishes what part of the crust we arrive on; human response can dramatically change what is possible. God does not always get God's will done, even though God is always involved.

For Cobb, the Logos is the primordial nature of God, giving the initial aim to each moment of becoming. God, with a full knowledge of beauty, truth, and goodness—and with a taste for adventure and zest—receives the previous moment, understands it completely, and then offers initial aims for the next moment.

Since mutual indwelling is natural for God and the world, then the variable for bringing both God and a person together in perfect harmony is *faithfulness*. Nothing has to be subtracted to get God into the event, for the event is already taking place in God. The human role is to embody and give existence to the insistence of God's Word. At the heart of this dynamic is an image of divine self-investment: in each moment, God gives the Word to the world and then receives back into God all that the world becomes. You could say that this giving of Godself to the world is incarnational. When we are aware of and respond to God's call, then God's will is done on earth and God is made flesh.

I love understanding Jesus as the fully faithful one over the sinless one. It's more invitational than burdensome.

THE BISHOP

The Incarnation of the Incarnation-al God

One of my biggest frustrations after learning about all the christological controversies covered in this chapter is how the conclusion seemed divorced from the source. There was the philosophical problem of the hypostatic union, but, beyond that, the Christologies all seemed to describe a God who was up-there and out-there for millennia, then finally decided to show up in Jesus. An incarnation-by-divine-invasion relativized the humanity of Jesus and the history of Israel. To me, Cobb's doctrine of God made much more sense of the God described in Scripture. Plus, seeing Jesus' faithfulness as the key to understanding his divinity not only coheres more with the Gospels but also rejects the subtraction method. The question that lingered for me was whether an incarnational understanding of God was compatible with identifying Jesus as *the* incarnation.

If you take one route, then the life of Jesus was a happy accident, a series of contingent events in which Jesus' faithfulness to God resulted in an expression of God's Word. Under this interpretation, the life of Jesus would be derivative and secondary to the eternal Word. Unlike other liberal theologians, Cobb insists that the Logos was uniquely present in Jesus. The difference between the presence of the Logos in Jesus and its presence in other humans is not a matter of degree, but of their structure of existence.

Not only was Jesus fully faithful to the lure of God before him, but he was uniquely so. Unlike most of us, for whom the call of God comes from outside of ourselves, for Jesus it was internal, a part of who he was. Cobb comes to this robust affirmation of God in Jesus by highlighting two features of his ministry: the authority that Jesus demonstrated, which leaped beyond the prophets and offended the pious of his day, and Jesus' intimacy with the God he knew as Abba. Together, they signal a person whose words and deeds are expressive of God in a direct way. Far from the Logos subtracting from his humanity, it is in and through the fullness of his humanity that Jesus is the Christ.

Creative transformation is Cobb's image of God's redeeming work in the world. Through the creative, adventurous novelty of God, the dead-ends and death-dealing paths of the world are given new possibilities. In Jesus Christ, creative transformation was on the move, and it continues to move as the advent of a new way to be human is initiated. The Word of the cross is not one of condemnation but rather one of invitation; it allows the believer to see the reality of themselves and the world, to

turn toward Christ, and to partner in the creative transformation of the world.

When the Logos/Word came into Jesus, it didn't push
out another, human part of him. In fact, only through the
ongoing call-and-response between God and the world
did the incarnation become possible. What this means for
Jesus specifically is that his identity and vocation, and the
presence of God moving through him, did not happen in a
bubble. Instead, it was the product of the Word's ongoing
relationship with the people of Israel that set the conditions for Jesus' faithfulness.

The Diversity of the Word

Of course, John Cobb's answer is only one response to the
predicament of Christology. I just think his is particularly
zesty. He takes modern science and our contemporary
worldview seriously, and puts them in conversation with
traditional views of Christ. For some liberals, his Christology is too high because it continues to affirm *the* incarnation of God in Christ. Others will argue that it is too
low because it minimizes the *person* of Jesus in light of the
Logos and fails to produce a Trinitarian vision of God.
While his Logos Christology is clearly one from above,
beginning with the Word's involvement in every moment
of creation, the particularity of Jesus is descriptively built
from below through his own faithfulness.

And it's that very particularity that poses another
problem for us. One of the toughest issues for contemporary Christians is that of religious pluralism. How can
you can affirm the presence of God at work in your own
tradition and not dismiss the same potential in others?

Particularity and exclusivity are very much baked into the logic of any monotheistic faith: if there's only one God, then the temptation is either to make an absolutist claim about the truth of your own religion or to relativize every religion to avoid being judgmental.

It was easier to be an exclusivist about Christ in earlier times, especially when diversity in your high school meant that some kids were plain old Baptists while others were Free Will Baptists. But now we live in a globalized world, and most of us think that the accident of someone's birth should not dictate their eternal destiny. If God is at least as nice as Jesus, then God has to have been busy pursuing all people in all places with divine love. That's just how Abba rolls.

Pluralists often imagine the religious journey as a trek up a mountain. Each religious tradition starts at the base of a different part of the mountain, but as you climb you become closer and closer to the saints in other traditions. While the top of the mountain is hidden from view in the clouds, the mystics in each tradition describe a thin place near the top where all the paths meet. The problem I have with this picture of religion is that it ends up relativizing the very place one comes to know God. It's ultimately an easy

THE DEACON

I still haven't read a Cobb book, but I've found Bob Marley and my COEXIST bumper sticker to be helpful in facing the dilemma of pluralism as well.

way to tell people that they are as right or as wrong about God as anyone else is. While I'm confident that God is present in other traditions, I am also confidently Christian.

I've found John Cobb helpful in facing the dilemma of pluralism as well. For example, he does not want the person of Jesus to usurp the primordial identity of the Logos. But he doesn't buy the idea of "anonymous Christians," the concept that some people have unknowingly responded to the spirit of Christ/Logos even though they've never heard of Jesus. Instead, Cobb posits a more complex view: the diversity of religions and their historical integrity demand multiple structures of existence originating from the Logos. Get that? I told you it was complex.

Just as the Christian tradition can be seen as the fruit of thousands of years of God relating to one particular people, so too can we view other religious traditions as locations where God has invested Godself. The wisdom of a tradition is not derivative of Christianity, nor subservient to it, but is developed in its own community, people, and history. Many religions have developed in response to the Logos, *and* (not but) in Christ the Word became flesh.

Affirming the authenticity of multiple religious traditions in unison seems hard on the surface, but we regularly make similar statements about other relationships in our lives. Think of the sheer number of variables involved in a couple celebrating a fiftieth anniversary. If one had gone to a different school or had moved to a different city, then the very relationship that has centered and grounded their entire lives would never have happened. Their love was an "accident of history," but for them it was much more. If we're able to admit the accidental nature of their relationship and simultaneously dignify the authenticity of its intimacy and history, then we should be able to do so for other traditions, even as we stand within Christianity. No one tells their friend, "You and your spouse can't really be in love because my spouse and I possess the One True Love." Love isn't a zero-sum game. Both can be true, and both can be different. We do not *possess* love, and we cannot *possess* God. After all, it's not the accidents of history that create love, but rather the relationship formed through those accidents that solidify it.

In the end, Cobb's creative proposal seeks to be faithful to the whole of the tradition while tackling some of the more gnawing contemporary questions. It's Cobb's answer, and I like it. But it's not the only one. There are about as many answers to the predicaments of Christology as there are theologians with PhDs. This chapter has been an attempt to show some of the modern challenges to the doctrine of Christ and to highlight one theological gambit to overcome those challenges—it's not perfect, but it is fresh and thought provoking.

Remember, this is all about brewing your own faith. I'm only trying to help you make sure that your beer doesn't go skunky while it's fermenting.

7

Turning Jesus Down

I was a sophomore in college on September 11, 2001. My roommate Michael and I were getting ready for the school's mandatory chapel service when the first plane crashed into the World Trade Center. Between the first and second plane hitting, little sense could be made of what, at least on the news, seemed to be a human error. Once we realized these were part of a coordinated attack, the suffering and tragedy experienced by those involved became an existential threat. And all of a sudden, my unexamined and unconscious place within America came to the surface of my psyche. I was filled with anger and a desire for vengeance, and I was ready to act.

As we walked to chapel, I was thinking about how we, the United States, would and should respond. I remember nothing of the chapel service. Anticipating war at nineteen years of age can be distracting. Afterward, there was a prayer circle out front. Not wanting to be out-Jesused

133

by my classmates, I joined a few dozen students in a giant circle, each praying aloud, in turn. They prayed for those who died, those who lost friends and family, those who fight to protect our country, and the heroes working to rescue people trapped beneath the rubble. It made perfect sense to pray then, joining hands with all the different Christians on campus.

After thirty minutes or so, people began to leave, and others joined the circle. My roommate took off and I followed; we walked back to our dorm room. He was clearly frustrated, and I assumed it was the rather poor theology displayed in a number of the prayers. At a time like this, hearing that "God is in control and has a plan for everything" is infuriating. For Michael, though, that wasn't the issue at all. In a voice of pure exhaustion, having tolerated all the pompous religiosity he could handle, he said, "You just don't get it. All those people were sitting there praying 'in Jesus' name,' and the *one thing* he said for such a day as this wasn't even mentioned. Jesus told us to *pray for our enemies*! The moment that second plane hit the building we knew we had enemies, and we should know what Jesus told us to do. He didn't say, 'Pray for protection, pray for your troops, pray for your president.' He said, 'Pray for your enemies.'"

I was silent. He was right, and I didn't care.

In the days to come, we talked for hours on end about the ethical predicament facing Christians as the drumbeat for war began. From President Bush's speech at Ground Zero, to TV networks constantly replaying the planes' impact, to the passage of the Patriot Act, there was a growing anticipation of release. We longed for something to reestablish our standing and place in the world—we longed for the peace of war.

Recently, I've tried explaining this feeling to kids in my youth ministry, and they just don't get it. The world I was born into, post–Cold War and pre-9/11, is over.

Vietnam definitely shaped my generation. Sadly, we forgot.

THE BISHOP

The first night the United States and friends began bombing Afghanistan, the men's dorm lobby was full. All the draftable fellas were breathing a sigh of relief as CNN replayed the videos of Tomahawk cruise missiles impacting the enemy (and their neighbors). It was cathartic. We even ordered pizza, like it was a sporting event! It's hard for me to think back to those first few months and remember what it was like to be me—the torment and twisting in my soul. I knew my Jesus-quoting roommate was right, that my response, like that of so many Christians, was far from Jesus. I was fine with that. If you had told me then that the bombing I was treating like a Saturday afternoon movie would lead to the death of over twenty thousand Afghani citizens, I am not sure I would have cared.[1] Looking back, the energy and creativity I put into defending our military response and the existential release the initial onslaught brought me remains disturbing.

My perspective was continually challenged by others. After an hour-long conversation with the campus minister, he asked, "Do you really think Jesus would be comfortable with what you are saying on his behalf? There are a bunch of reasons for the most powerful military to attack people that threaten them. But I don't think Jesus is one of them."

THE DEACON

It's amazing how many American Christians had no one challenge their ideology.

That night I had a crazy dream. In it, I was talking with Reinhold Niebuhr, the twentieth century's greatest American ethicist, about the contemporary political situation, when someone looking like Bob Marley showed up. The thing was, it wasn't Bob, it was Jesus. All Jesus said were direct quotes from the New Testament. I woke up drenched in sweat. The conversation was unresolved, but I knew that I couldn't stay the same.

THE ELDER

What kind of person has dreams like this?

My theological education and my fifteen years in ministry have all been after 9/11. It's hard to imagine a situation where the confluence of questions coming out of that day don't shape my thinking. So many issues thrust themselves onto us, each one demanding significant reflection for Christians. After 9/11, I came to realize just how much of my own understanding of Jesus was tied to my identity as a straight, white, middle-class, firstborn son of a preacher in the Bible Belt. Now, post-9/11, my passion for God and my ever-present skepticism have to learn to live together.

That skepticism always leads me directly to Christology. Others may begin with a doctrine of God, the End Times, or the Holy Spirit, but I have always tried to begin with Christology. The reason is personal. In college, after 9/11, I had a period when I doubted God's existence, and I wondered what community or narrative could do any good in the face of all the global crises. Intellectually, I was busy deconstructing Christology, and I was digging the historical Jesus, especially his critique of the political order.

Not knowing if the idea of God was reasonable, or even if things like meaning, purpose, and value were more than stories we tell ourselves, I remember thinking, *if anything is true, this radical Jew should be true: if there is a deity, the only one that could help is one like this.* It's as if my inner skeptic said, "Who knows about the metaphysics, historicity, or human projection involved in this story? It's aesthetically compelling—it's so beautiful that it's worth giving your life to."

And that's how, because of Jesus, I stuck around long enough to work things out with God—at least for now.

Does God Give a Crap?

"If you live a while, you will finally ask a scary enough question to become a real theologian." That's what a Benedictine monk said to me once at the end of a weeklong retreat. He said it like a koan, smirked, and then said goodbye and left. We'd talked about God and life all week, so I wasn't sure exactly what he meant. It wasn't until life stomped all over my soul that I figured it out.

Why would it take going through my own personal hell to become a real theologian? What is gained from going through a period of darkness, anguish, and suffering that, at least theologically, isn't available in books? Until I'd had that experience, I refused to believe all that was necessary to become a theologian. Now, I think not only that it's necessary to have life beat a scary question out of you but also that Jesus needed to ask a scary question if God was ever going to understand us and redeem the world.

Jürgen Moltmann was the theologian who gave me the courage to ask if God really gives a crap. The twentieth century saw more human slaughter than anyone could have anticipated. The growth of democratic nation-states, the free market, and the Industrial Revolution did not bring a century of peace, but one of war and unimaginable suffering. After Hiroshima, Nagasaki, and Auschwitz, viable Christian theology became a problematic endeavor. At no other time in history were humans more aware of just how vile we could be as a species. To talk about a loving and sovereign God seemed more and more laughable. If the church could not address the actual world and its very real horrors, then it should have just shut up.

No theologian more directly faced the challenge that evil and suffering put on theology than Jürgen Moltmann, a German soldier and an Allied prisoner of war in World War II. For Moltmann, Christian theology had long ignored its very center: the cross. In his theology of the cross, Moltmann insists that Jesus' own experience of god-forsakenness on the cross should ground all thinking about God. Moltmann found a brother in Jesus in the cry of dereliction, "My God, my God, why have you forsaken me?"[2]

In that statement, Moltmann heard Jesus dare to protest against God in the midst of suffering. While he went on to develop some amazing theology, the simple yet powerful recognition that Jesus knew and shared the ugliest and worst of our experience was Moltmann's epiphany. The first time I read Moltmann with a group of students, one of them summarized him by saying, "In Christ, God not only gave a shit, but got *in* our shit to make beauty out of it."

For most of the church's history, the suffering of Jesus on the cross was primarily seen as part of God's atoning work, not as an event within the life of God. In order to preserve the perfection of God, it's anathema to say that God could experience suffering. But here's the thing: this notion of divine perfection is not based on the Bible's portrayal of God, nor is it logically connected to what we know about Jesus. In order to preserve this nonbiblical notion of divine perfection, the historical church has quarantined the pathos of God in the Hebrew Scriptures and hermetically sealed God's essence to protect it from the suffering of Jesus.

Why would the church want to keep the cross from their understanding of God?

THE ACOLYTE

The pathos of God, a concept Moltmann found in Jewish theologian Abraham Heschel, springs from God's overwhelming commitment to the people of Israel. There's a vulnerability and investment in people that makes the historical process matter within God and to God. In the Bible's prophetic books, for example, we find a God who cares about the plight of the poor and oppressed—a God who is set against the godlessness of the world. God's passion is displayed in compassion for others; God shares in their sufferings and rejoices in their joys.

For Moltmann, a God who does not suffer or change is not really God, but a demon! God is the one who cares. The strength of this assertion comes not only from Moltmann's own experience but from the cross of Christ. When theologians have traditionally asked what suffers on the cross of Jesus, the answer is based on the two natures of Jesus: his full humanity and his full divinity. The usual response is that the experience of suffering and godforsakenness was limited to the humanity of Jesus, as it was incompatible with his divinity. In stark contrast, inspired by the pathos of God, Moltmann locates the suffering of the cross in the very heart of God.

The cross of Jesus must be a Trinitarian event. In fact, for Moltmann, the entire logic of the Trinity and the meaning of Christian theology must be worked out from the cross. When Christians speak of God, we must not use a generic concept of an infinite deity. The word *God* is defined in Christ, the one who was crucified and raised. This means not only that God suffers with Jesus but that the divine life is changed, the pathos of God is embodied in Jesus, and the eschatological shape of the divine life is revealed. The crucified-but-risen one reveals God's presence in history, participating in our suffering and promising us new life.

On the cross, the Son dies abandoned by the one he called Abba. But, in his rejection, suffering, abandonment, and execution, the Son is not alone, for he has become the brother of all the abandoned. This brother of the forsaken is also the eternal Son, who, in his identification with them, also brings the presence of God. For Moltmann, only the crucified God can be the good God of the crucified people. God's relationship to the cross is not through the Son alone but through all three persons: the Father is moved to intense grief by this event, as the one who can truly know the death of the Son; the Spirit preserves and gives new life and hope to this relationship on the other side of death.

The triune God does not reside in heaven, at a remove from humankind. On the cross of Jesus, God has identified with the guilty and the forsaken, overcoming our alienation from God and bringing us the promise of our own future in the divine life. In one of my favorite passages, Moltmann puts it this way,

> All human history, however much it may be determined by guilt and death, is taken up into this "history of God," i.e. into the Trinity, and integrated into the future of the "history of God." There is no suffering which in this history of God is not God's suffering; no death which has not been God's death in the history of Golgotha. Therefore there is no life, no fortune and no joy

which have not been integrated by his history into eternal life, the eternal joy of God.[3]

The image of God and God's relationship to history must be redefined, according to Moltmann. Just as the future of the cross-dead Christ was not death itself but life in God, so too is the future of the world in God. This is not an image of hunky-dory universalism that ignores the reality of history and the tragedy of our world—no! God is not denying violence and suffering but sharing in it, and thereby reconciling it.

What blew my mind the first time I read Moltmann was this: Jesus Christ is the human face of God, and, without him, Moltmann would reject God in general because God would have rejected all those discarded throughout history's bloody past. It is only through the message of the

---

THE BISHOP

For some, belief in God comes easily, and for others, like Moltmann, it's really difficult. I think the church is blessed by both.

---

kin-dom, Jesus' suffering on the cross, and the promise of God through the resurrection that Moltmann could believe in a deity, let alone a God who is love.

Suffering and death stand as a potent witness against God's existence. Only a crucified God can justify speaking the name of God again.

Yeah, we've learned
it's probably best to
avoid the contradiction
of placing God

THE ELDER

everywhere but on the cross. The Holy
Spirit's presence has to be in the suffering
and the death, or the God we speak of is
unfamiliar with the full human experience

Jesus Was a Dude, but Is God?

The answer is no. God is not a man, but Jesus was. God
does not have a penis, and this isn't news to theologians.
Throughout church history, it's been clear that God was
never a man and that to superimpose a gender on God is
to misunderstand the very definition of God. Once you
start discussing God's gender, then no matter where the
conversation goes, you are assuming that even the question itself is unintelligible. The mystery and transcen-
dence of God puts God categorically beyond a discussion
of genders and body parts.

While God's mystery precludes having a gender, this
hasn't stopped the church from using almost exclusively
masculine language for God. This language is dominant
not only in our biblical texts but also within the patriarchal cultures from which they came and the ones in which
they are interpreted. Given that men were the heads of the
church, culture, state, and home, it's to be expected that
this language would dominate our religious communities.

Throw in the fact that Jesus was a dude and called God "Father," and you've got all the material needed to avoid responsible language for God.

The language we use for God has real power. "God" functions symbolically to inscribe a religious community's sense of mystery, its worldview, the structure of its institutions, and each person's particular place within it. Because language is that powerful, shaping our material existence regardless of how abstract or ambiguous it may seem, it's essential for Christians to pay attention to the language we use for God. And nothing demonstrates the powerful legacy of unexamined discourse for the divine more than patriarchy. Long after our country and many of its churches have officially recognized the equal dignity of all people, it's tragic that the power and privilege of patriarchy still persists. It was Elizabeth Johnson, a Catholic feminist theologian, who first helped me learn to identify it, and recognizing it significantly changed how I speak as a minister and how Alecia and I teach our children to pray.

When Elgin was born, we committed ourselves to praying the Lord's Prayer before bed each night. When we do, we always say "Our Mother," hoping that prioritizing feminine imagery for God might minimize the effects of a church that ignored God's symbolic power for years. What we soon discovered was that the inertia of patriarchy is strong. When Elgin was four, I heard from his Sunday School teacher that he corrected a peer, explaining that the Lord's Prayer begins, "Our Mother." A year and a half later, as I was putting Elgin to bed, he said, "Dad, can we do a real prayer and call God a man?" I was shocked and taken aback.

It wasn't until his sister Khora was born that Elgin changed the way he felt about God's gender. One night, after reading the story of Deborah the judge of Israel for the hundredth time, he told me unsolicited that "God does not have a penis or a vagina, so we can pray with both or none. I bet Khora likes Mom for God and Jesus is her brother like me. Maybe Khora will tell armies what to do like Deborah. I think she should say, 'Don't actually kill people. Go eat cupcakes!'" I started laughing hard and suggested that we put that in our prayer for the evening— *stop killing and eat more cupcakes*.

The cupcake foreign policy plan sounds wonderful.

THE ACOLYTE

Consider how the language for God functions in our imaginations. In *She Who Is*, Elizabeth Johnson gives one of the most powerful and sustained theological treatments of patriarchy that I've ever read. She helped me see that when we use exclusively masculine language for God, there are multiple problems. Without feminine imagery alongside the masculine, it can become idolatrous. Moreover, exclusively masculine God-talk is easily appropriated by patriarchy to justify itself and to diminish women's dignity. When attempting to move the conversation about God's gender forward, Christians fighting for equality will always have to answer for the christological reality that Jesus was a dude who called God daddy.

How one deals with the maleness of Jesus is important for addressing the silent powers of patriarchy. Johnson does this by first locating the places in which Christology unwittingly serves to oppress women, and then she develops a robust understanding of Christology, seeing Jesus as Wisdom's child. She highlights that the imperial powers that came to dominate the church twisted and appropriated the story of Jesus into a legitimating narrative for a patriarchal worldview. As the church became more and more comfortable with the dominant culture, it also became more accepting of its unjust structures, like its patriarchal household codes and slavery.

THE DEACON

This is where the progressive Christian churches need to "rise up against the man."

The maleness of Jesus has facilitated two primary perversions from the liberating message that Jesus came to embody and teach. First, it's been used to justify a patriarchal image of God, drawing on the Father-Son metaphor in Jesus' own preaching and his calling of twelve male disciples, then extending his maleness to the Logos itself. The historical Jesus was very much at the forefront of women's empowerment in the first century, and Jesus' own understanding of Abba and the kin-dom criticized the dominating patriarchal system of his day. The most important theological issue for Johnson is that of the Logos. If the Word of God was made flesh in Jesus, a man, then it didn't take much for theologians (almost all male themselves) to see his gender as part of the divine disclosure.

If the use of Jesus to enshrine the dude into the divine weren't problematic enough, Jesus' genitalia have also perverted the church's understanding of humanity. If the one in whom we are reconciled to God and the one to whom we are called to imitate is male, then it's not a stretch to think that one gender is superior to the other. It may seem that these observations are a bit dramatic, especially when so many of our denominations are now ordaining women and putting them in leadership positions. But even though women make up the majority of Protestant church members, the number who end up preaching in a pulpit remains small, hovering around 10 percent.[4]

There's a reason churches will ordain and train women ministers and then continue to call only men to the ministry, and it's not talent. As one lay leader put it to me, "I would feel bad bringing a woman to preach as a senior minister candidate [in my congregation]. It's not that I wouldn't support her, it's just there would be so much work to do before she would ever be heard. It's probably best to have women preach in pulpits where people can listen." I didn't doubt this person's honesty and sincerity, but it made me wonder what has to be done to change things when even advocates for change protect the pockets of patriarchy in their own congregations.

Have You Invited Sophia into Your Heart?

In order to shatter the androcentric agenda coming from the misappropriation of the Logos tradition, Johnson uses the image of Sophia, the "Wisdom of God," in the Hebrew

Scriptures. Wisdom is strikingly similar in both function and purpose to the Logos in John. In the book of Proverbs, Wisdom is present with God prior to creation and she participates in the joy of God creating.[5] In the Wisdom of Solomon, Wisdom is described as Mother and the fashioner of all things, and then you get this powerful image:

> For she is a reflection of eternal light,
> a spotless mirror of the working of God,
> and an image of his goodness.
> Although she is but one, she can do all things,
> and while remaining in herself, she renews all
>   things;
> in every generation she passes into holy souls
> and makes them friends of God, and prophets;
>   or God loves nothing so much as the person
> who lives with wisdom.[6]

Jesus himself applied the image of Wisdom when he said, "The Son of Man came eating and drinking, and they say, 'Look, a glutton and a drunkard, a friend of tax collectors and sinners!' Yet wisdom is vindicated by her deeds."[7] Here, Jesus sees his own embodiment of the kin-dom as the very action of Wisdom. Paul calls Christ-crucified the "power of God and the wisdom of God," and in the Gospel of John, Jesus says, "I came that they may have life, and have it abundantly."[8] As Johnson points out, the Logos of God is here echoing the very promise of the Wisdom of God in Scripture to give life to all who seek it out.[9] All these elements of the Wisdom tradition serve not to eliminate all masculine language about Jesus but to show that the masculinity of Jesus is not required theologically to establish his identity as the Christ.

The bigger the Christ
the better.

THE DEACON

Looking at the ministry of Sophia-Jesus through the paradigm of Wisdom, the shape and character of Jesus' words and deeds become the location for understanding the definition of God's wisdom. The ministry of Jesus-Sophia announced God's all-inclusive love and unleashed an anticipatory vision of liberation for all the oppressed. The preaching, welcoming, and prophetic confrontation of Jesus-Sophia led to his death, as it had for others before him. Yet for Johnson, the dying and rising of Christ is to be seen as the victory of God's shalom.

The resurrection is not only a vindication of the ministry of Jesus, but also a pledge for the future of all victimized people. The crucified and risen Jesus, as the Wisdom of God, now proclaims the truth of divine justice and the transformative power of Sophia over death. The cross of Jesus is set against male dominance precisely because the crucified Christ is the antithesis of the patriarchal male. Instead, the crucifixion functions as a call to struggle for liberation; the cross is a symbol of the kenosis, or complete emptying, of the entire idea of patriarchy altogether.[10]

Differentiating Jesus-Sophia from a historical individual allowed the early church to participate in this same Spirit. As the body of Christ, we are called to live within the spirit and mission of Sophia-Jesus, regardless of gender. This does not mean that Johnson relativizes the incarnation, for she believes that God's indwelling Spirit took on a new intensity in God's self-revelation in Jesus. The incarnation cannot be identified with Jesus alone, but must also be seen as the symbol for God's desired mutual communion of heaven and earth. Sophia was incarnate in Jesus, and the divine mystery revealed in Jesus is that of Sophia. The incomprehensible God is made known in new and intimate ways in Jesus, and this God continues to be found in communities who live in and for the same liberating Spirit.

When the ministry of Jesus is turned into filler material before the big finale on the cross, the inclusivity and prophetic thrust of his life are chopped off. By connecting the ministry of Jesus to the Wisdom of God, Johnson insists that it remains the wisdom of the church. Jesus spent his life being obedient not to religion but to love, which he embodied through compassion, forgiveness, and justice—that is true religion for Jesus and Sophia's agenda. This means that God should not be seen as the big male authoritarian judge in the sky demanding obedience. This patriarchal image of God is not bad only for women, but for men too. It creates an impoverished spirituality built on fear, power, and divine demands. Who wants that when Wisdom has come to give abundant life?!

I was on staff for almost seven years at a large congregation of the United Church of Christ. Theoretically, the UCC is the most progressive Protestant denomination in the country, but when the use of gender-inclusive language touched the doxology, the hymn of praise often sung after the offering during the service, for the first time, an insurgency of patriarchy was born. What's amazing is that the doxology wasn't changed to include feminine language. We kept the traditional language for the Trinity, "Father, Son, and Holy Ghost," but instead of "Praise Him all creatures," we sang "Praise God all creatures." One of the vocal opponents of the "radical neutering of God" visited my office in a huff. It was clear that he was impassioned and not interested in listening to me. I asked him if something about the change bothered him religiously, or if it was more the change in general?

To my surprise, he said, "Oh, I am upset religiously, and I just hate change in general. If you and I know that God isn't male, then why the hell should we change it? Of course, He's not a man. He's Spirit." I paused, then said, "Well, if that's the case, then tell me what's going on at church. You and I know that historic Christianity never intended God to become a man when She doesn't even have a gender. As a minister and a father, I get worried that many in the congregation may confuse the exclusivity of our use of language for genuine theological beliefs. Even if we know that masculinity isn't hiding behind the word *God*, it could come across that way." He promptly told me that he didn't care at all what was hiding behind God, or who had to stay in the closet, but that it was his church and he wasn't going to let it change. This experience reminded me of a favorite line from Johnson, who said, "The heart of the problem is not that Jesus was a man, but that more men are not like Jesus, insofar as patriarchy defines their self-identity and relationships."[11]

Well, bless his heart.

THE BISHOP

Asking Jesus Out of Your Heart, and Back In

The other day I was working on this book at my local coffee shop. When one of the regulars asked what I was typing, I told him. This clearly included an invitation to tell
me a twenty-minute story about his evangelical upbringing and how many "serious spiritual traumas" it left him
with. After hearing a horrendous story of religious manip-
ulation, fearmongering, and shaming, he asked me, "So
have you asked Jesus into your heart? I'm not judging, but
I spent the last decade trying to get him out." I ignored the
question and instead asked about his quest to get Jesus out
of his heart. What he proceeded to describe were painful
periods where he had to part ways with Jesus because he
needed something else to be true.

Surprisingly, what he needed to be true were things
I thought fit right into the Jesus story. For example, his
brother came out as gay to their family and got married
three years later. Inviting his brother over for Thanks-
giving and attending his wedding meant that he had
to kick Jesus out. He and I know each other from local
Sierra Club meet-ups, so knowing we both care about
the ecological crisis, he said that when he admitted to
himself the veracity of climate change, he had to kick
Jesus out again because you can't get people to pray away
the CO_2. He also described very painful personal experiences, all of which he thought required having less of
Jesus around.

When he finished sharing, I told him how grateful
I was for his vulnerability. He asked if I would pray for
him, and I agreed. Then he said, "What are you going

to pray for?" I didn't exactly know, so I paused. Then he said something that was so awesome I told him that it was going to have to be in the book. He said, "When you pray, tell God that my heart needs to grow. I want one big enough to care about the world, be honest about my struggles, and still have JC around. Maybe God could rock my heart like the Grinch's."

A week or so later, we saw each other again, and I asked how his heart growth was going. He said, "You know, I might just have to get myself a Bible and find a church again. I've got a bunch of questions. It's really weird, but I think the issue for some Christians, if they grew up like me, is they think you only have to ask Jesus into your heart and then he's there keeping everything else out. What if what Jesus really wants is to grow your heart so more and more can get in?" I smiled and said, "Thank you, Reverend, for my next Christmas sermon, 'How the Grinch Did Christmas.'"

I've been trying to figure out a way to describe my own ongoing relationship with Jesus. When I think back to all the different images and understandings of Jesus I've had, and probably defended with gusto, I recognize that we all need room in our hearts for the Jesuses we have encountered and will continue to encounter in various forms. Our understanding of Jesus should continue to grow within us, in the same way that over time we deepen our understanding of any living person we love. Part of the challenge is being willing to let go of a Jesus that's too small and to make room for more. It's been a long time since I asked someone if they had asked Jesus into their heart, but I believe we could do some good as a church if we asked about making more room. It's only because I had the space to ask the questions that I could have learned from Moltmann and Johnson.

THE ELDER

In effect, we are creating space for a Christ to be born who, as the story goes, invaded a world in which there was "no room in the inn."

8

The Skeptic and the Believer

When I teach confirmation class, I tend to make a big deal about questions. The process ultimately boils

Ha, Tripp and his process references.

THE DEACON

down to the one Jesus put to his disciples: "Who do you say that I am?"[1] It's my contention, however, that the questions surrounding that question are just as important as the initial question itself. You can easily answer a question and never understand what it's really about. As a church we can even repeat "the correct" answers to avoid taking the question Jesus posed seriously. Seriously attending to questions not only leads to a more passionate church, but one that has something of substance to say.

There are two theological temptations to avoid. Conservative Christians are tempted to regurgitate answers to questions the world isn't asking. Liberal Christians often have theological laryngitis, aware of the right questions but unable to avoid answers that deflate God.[2] Moving

THE ELDER

Sermonic regurgitations may be horrible, but they are profitable.

forward will require us to speak out about our convictions with declarative sentences. I believe we need to talk with passion and conviction about God, and especially about Jesus Christ. The thing is, we don't acquire passionate convictions by memorizing them. They are hard fought and earned as we carry our questions and follow after Jesus.

Jesus was quite possibly the most annoying theology professor of all time. Someone would ask him a good question, and he'd dodge it by telling a parable. Although he didn't interpret many of the parables, he did interpret the Torah in ways that begged for embodiment. To figure out much of what Jesus was teaching, his followers had to become part of the community and its mission. Only in walking, talking, serving, healing, and empowering others did the meaning of Jesus' theological riddle-stories become evident. That's why, during confirmation, the students and I slowly go through a single Gospel and come up with experiments in living to practice the teachings of Jesus. As we do, I have them write down on notecards the biggest question they have each week and drop it in the "Big God Question" bowl. Because I'm a bit wordy, I usually answered only one or two per session, but we all came to understand that it's the asking of the question, not the answer, that's important.

At the end of the confirmation process, the students write an answer to the question Jesus asked his disciples. They read and share them with each other, and when they are done, I pull out the bowl of questions. After reading them, I say, "I bet most of these questions you asked, you don't need to ask anymore. I bet your friends asked some questions you were scared to ask, and you asked some your parents wouldn't even understand. Some of these questions, though, were not answered, and they still need to be asked. I want you to ask them and keep asking them. But as you do, remember that the place Christians ask these questions and where we sometimes even get the answers—if they are to be found—is in the community of Christ.

I love when the body of Christ brings its questions to the church and answers them as they serve together.

THE BISHOP

"Christ explicitly promised to be in three places: in community, at the communion table, and among the oppressed. If we want answers, we know where to go. Answers found outside communities are personal speculations. Away from the table, our answers miss the abundance of grace. If we are distanced from and ignorant of the oppressed, our answers become idolatrous shields for our own power and privilege." My goal here is not to answer all of the students' questions—a real temptation to a nerd like me—but to help them realize that proclaiming Jesus as the Christ is so much more than a cognitive act. To call Jesus the Christ, to call him Lord, is way more like falling in love than like solving a math equation.

THE ACOLYTE

Why do so many Christians act like it's a math equation? Geometry has nothing on love.

Plus, if you pause for a moment and think back through your own life and the different convictions you have held along the way, there's rarely a bunch of steady and unwavering convictions. The tragedies and joys of life affect our understanding of God, and so do the questions we carry and the places from which we ask them. In this last chapter, I want to talk about two places where my own reflection on Jesus was radically challenged and opened up to new insights.

Jesus from the Underside of History

The first time I read Jon Sobrino's *Jesus the Liberator*, my mind was blown. As you know by now, there was a time when I was obsessed with research on the historical Jesus. Coming to see him in his historical context radically changed my understanding of Jesus and the shape of my faith. If I had never realized how politically charged his own ministry was, I would have continued to spiritualize and personalize his prophetic and communal vision.

Yes! When the vision gets bigger the gospel gets zestier!

THE DEACON

The quest for the historical Jesus not only changed the way I understood Jesus and read the Gospels, but it also opened up a new avenue for doing Christology— Christology *from below*. What better way to engage the Christian tradition than through a robust account of Jesus himself? Here's the thing: Sobrino develops a Christology from below by beginning with the historical Jesus but also insisting that in light of Jesus' historical situation and location, we cannot ignore the voices of those in similar situations today. As a Jesuit priest in El Salvador, he brought the experience of those on the underside of our world in Latin America into my theological imagination. It is easy to make Jesus into a generic theological platitude and divorce him from his historicity and materiality, and that's what I'd done.

Sobrino argues that Jesus treats the poor and oppressed with a clear preference. This principle of Catholic social teaching sees Christ as a liberator. Sobrino describes a shift from seeing the suffering of Christ as a symbol to

THE ELDER

The "preferential option for the poor" was established in 1979 at a gathering of the Latin American Episcopal Conference in Puebla. Pope Francis has reenergized this concept.

be interpreted to understanding it as a protest against the suffering of oppressed people. To unpack this, he begins by articulating a nuanced understanding of the kingdom of God. While Jesus does not provide a simple definition of the kingdom, it was for him a life-determining reality within which God was present.

God never appears as God-in-Godself. Sobrino insists that if you read the New Testament, you will see that God is always present, working and active, but always within the network of relations and through people. The kingdom is the final reality where the God who gives Godself to history meets a history that has become exactly what God wants for it. In order to understand how good this news is, you have to see it from the perspective of those to whom it was addressed—namely, the poor and oppressed.

The kingdom of God, which Sobrino calls "the reign," is brought by God's initiative to and for the world, but it demands a conversion of the listener. While God's offer of love is for all, it does not come to everyone in the same way. The reign of God was primarily for the poor, both those in economic poverty and those with a lack of moral dignity. Those who take life's necessities for granted will not hear the news of the coming kingdom, which seeks to establish and enable basic human dignity for all humans, with its intended enthusiastic goodness. It was true in Jesus' day just as it's true in ours that the author of salvation *for all* makes different demands *of each*. Properly understood, salvation is always of someone from something, and this means the systemic and institutional challenges to the kingdom cannot be ignored.

So God isn't just saving us for God but for one another?

THE ACOLYTE

Sobrino portrays the ministry of Jesus not only as the proclamation of God's reign, but also as the prophetic unmasking of the antikingdom. In Jesus' encounters with oppression, he insists that the people's needs trump ceremonial perfection. To love God is to practice goodwill toward the oppressed. God cannot be used to justify any form or structure of oppression. Thus, to encounter Jesus is to unmask the antikingdom and its structures of sin. These structures of oppression are usually based on an idol, such as wealth or religious vanity. Jesus opposes the rich directly because of the offensive abundance they possess in contrast to the inhuman poverty of others. Because riches work against the poor, they work against God, and they are a relational problem for the rich on both counts. Riches become an idol because they distract the person, demand allegiance, and inspire acts against God—namely, the dehumanizing of others. Sobrino observes that our economic interconnectedness allows the rich to sacrifice the poor on the altar of their wealth without even being aware they're doing it. I remember the shock of realizing

THE BISHOP

This demonstrates the need for the church to not only preach justice but educate and empower the people toward everyday justice.

the horrendous working conditions for those who harvest the tomatoes I purchase each week. To discover that one more cent per pound meant the workers received a fair wage blew my mind. It also taught me not to assume the system has a conscience.

Connecting the radical message of Jesus in his historical context to our own historical situation is challenging and even threatening. In fact, Sobrino points out that it is much easier for the theologians of the affluent to engage atheism with a reasoned argument for God's existence than to deal with the idolatry that runs rampant in their own hearts and churches and is sustained by the structures of today's anti-kingdom. Jesus does more than prove the existence of God to the intellectual and cultured skeptics; he shows what God is actually like, and he opposes all impostors.

The history of Jesus' ministry is the conflict between God and the idols. To understand the crucifixion of Jesus, you have to understand the primary conflict between Jesus and the oppressive centers of power. As he unmasked the idols and took the side of their sacrificed victims, Jesus

The fool may say in their heart that there is no God, but the idolatrous will say, "I need more cheddar."

THE ELDER

remained faithful to the one he called Abba. From the perspective of history, Jesus' death is the consequence of his life in mission against the antikingdom; from the perspective of theology, it is the result of a war of divinities. The divinity of Jesus should not distract the church from the battle of divinities—the challenge the God of Israel poses to the dehumanizing deities found in the political, economic, and religious structures of Jesus' time. Only in that challenge does the cross become the place at which the poor identify with the historical Jesus. The radical hope that Jesus had in the God he proclaimed is the same hope present in the crucified people on our planet today. In God's silence in the face of the suffering of both Jesus and the world's victims, God is discovered to be a fellow sufferer. God has chosen to become so invested and incarnate in history as to become affected by it.

Just like Alfred North Whitehead says, God is the great companion, a fellow sufferer who understands.

THE DEACON

To overcome sin, sin must be borne by God. Through God's sharing in the suffering of sin, God identifies with all who suffer injustice. This affirmation makes theology that is done apart from the victims of the world inherently problematic and even sub-Christian. The crucified God is found both in the crucified Son and the crucified people. If Moltmann developed a theology after Auschwitz, Sobrino is arguing for a theology *in* Auschwitz, recognizing the crucified people of our present global situation as Yahweh's suffering servant. Theology's job is not primarily to explain the world, but to unmask it.

In a sense, Jesus' own life does what religion had been trying to do from time immemorial through rituals, stories, and symbols. In the broken bodies of the crucified, God's love of the world and desire for human solidarity is finally made present. Ever since Sobrino revealed the unexamined privilege and its idolatrous allegiance in my own reflection on Jesus, I have tried to reckon with it. Figuring out what the idols are in our world is the easy part. The hard part has been coming to grips with my own love for other gods and the comfort and security my devotion to them brings.

The Lilies Considering Christ

If the place of the poor must be considered for genuine christological reflection today, so too must the plight of our planet. Pope Francis recently put the ecological crisis on the front burner of the church. He insists we recognize that the well-being of the poor and the planet are intertwined and under threat because of the reigning logic of our economy. As Christians, we need to ask ourselves what our faith in Jesus Christ has to say about the environment.

Or, as one of my confirmation students asked, "What does the good news about Jesus have to do with the impending destruction of our planet?" Sadly, the church hasn't offered much of a response.

Because this issue will shape so much of our future, theologians must take the challenge seriously. A number of the theologians we have already discussed are attempting to do just that. John Cobb was among the first theologians and philosophers to awaken to the ecological crisis. In the middle of his career, after having been prodded by his son, he shifted from doing doctrinal theology to doing interdisciplinary work to develop sustainable models of economy, community, government, energy, and more. Cobb believes that the church's mission must turn toward the ecological crisis.

At a recent denominational gathering of the UCC, Cobb noted that few churches are free to give themselves to the challenges that threaten life on the planet, and he challenged those present to "make your church's mission working with God for the salvation of the world." What more pertinent task could the Word of God, which comes to us each moment, be calling for? But Cobb's turn toward laypeople is what still challenges me most. The ecological crisis cannot be overcome by a powerful sermon or a brilliant theological treatise. God needs people in every vocation and center of power or influence advocating and acting on behalf of God's mission.

Over the years, Jon Sobrino has also reflected on the relationship between the poor and the planet. Since global capitalism ignores the well-being of both the planet and the poor, those committed to environmental justice and those committed to social justice can and should be allies. There is clear asymmetry between those violating the planet and those experiencing the consequences. The overwhelming majority of ecological destruction comes at the hands of the rich and powerful and benefits very few, while the negative impacts are borne by the poor and oppressed. This means that the voices of the crucified people can speak not only on Christ's behalf and their own behalf, but also on behalf of the groaning world. The salvation of the world must include both the liberation of the poor and the healing of the planet.

Jürgen Moltmann has also expanded his christological vision to address the ecological crisis more directly. Because the eschatological hope of the church includes all of creation, Moltmann argues that we must give nature the inherent value that God gives it. Practically, this means exchanging our rather hostile and utilitarian approach to the planet—one in which we dominate nature—for a mutually beneficial model of partnership in which we recognize ourselves not as above nature, but as part of nature. Relating to the world in more cooperative ways will require a transformation of our social and economic order by asserting and protecting of the rights of the earth. In *Ethics of Hope*, Moltmann observes that the prophet Isaiah even identifies the messiah as "a fruit of the earth."[3] This means that the earth is both the "mother of all the living" and the "womb of God."[4] By connecting God's activity of both creation and redemption to nature as a whole, he places the dignity of the planet at the heart of the gospel.

Among the theologians we have considered, Elizabeth Johnson has given the most attention to developing an ecological Christology in her book *Ask the Beasts: Darwin and the God of Love.*[5] The title of this book is taken from the book of Job, where God tells Job to "ask the beasts"—a question we don't ask very often. If we listen to their story, we will hear two things intertwined: Darwin's evolutionary theory and God's ongoing work in creation. For Johnson, God's co-creative endeavor with the world brought the complexity of life into existence. In light of God's continuous investment in creation, Johnson

---

Finally! Just a little bit of evolution makes me want to pay more attention when you keep dropping "creation."

THE ACOLYTE

---

turns again to her Wisdom Christology for an ecological perspective.

Johnson develops an understanding of what she calls "deep incarnation." Returning to the prologue of John, she notices that the Word/Wisdom of God became flesh—*sarx* in Greek. Among the different words available to the Johannine author to denote Jesus' materiality, he picked the most inclusive. *Sarx* is not simply a word for the human body, but actually a word for all material creation. This leads Johnson to recognize that what was being assumed in Christ was actually the entire story of life and all living things!

Deep Incarnation! Sarx! #SermonReady

THE DEACON

This ecological Christology goes deeper yet in the resurrection. A deep resurrection, the resurrection of *sarx* into the divine life, is a promise for the whole world. It's not a promise of escape, a promise just for our souls, or even only for humans. Instead, God has invested in the evolution of all life and in its entire redemption. There can be no stronger affirmation of the intrinsic value of nature than this.

Each of these theologians has spoken in a way that is responsible to the place in which we find ourselves on this planet. The way forward for the church must move us toward the poor and the planet. The needed change is not simply instrumental, like changing lightbulbs, eating less meat, or carpooling. Humanity, and in particular those in power, need a conversion, an existential change, the cultivation of new desires. We have changed how we live and relate to each other and the planet multiple times in human history. Now a change is needed more than ever, and it's my hope that Christ can once again call us to repentance. This will require theological attention to the symbolic. In our religious symbols, we communicate the shape of the relationships we will cultivate. Just as addressing patriarchy and the systematic oppression of the poor has required unmasking, reworking, and reviving the symbolic structure of Christianity, so too will the ecological crisis. As we start to wake up to the tragedy surrounding us, the theological challenge will be continuing to risk thinking after Christ—to wager putting our present system and the privilege and perks it provides before the cross.

The Skeptic and Believer

In permitting myself to be both a believer and a skeptic, I've discovered that I can be either a *believing skeptic* or a *skeptical believer*. The skeptical believer differentiates the passionate inwardness of one's faith in God from the particular questions and tentative conclusions one is thinking through. This doesn't mean the two in fact are separate or that faith is nonintellectual. On the contrary, there are subjective conditions—faith—needed to think theologically. The skeptical believer believes, but prays to Jesus, "Please help me with my unbelief." This single plea highlights the subjective nature of faith, for it is Jesus to whom you are coming with your unbelief. Why? Because it's in him that

---

Can you ask God to help your unbelief even if you aren't sure there's a God listening?

THE ACOLYTE

---

the Christian concept of God is crafted. Now, it shouldn't be hard to imagine someone taking their questions and doubts elsewhere; after all, Jesus was not an Ivy League academician. You come to Jesus because you believe he's the Christ—which is a bit crazy.

The believing skeptic, on the other hand, calls Jesus the Christ and identifies him as Lord, a belief that entails allegiance. This allegiance is not to blood, flag, or ideology, but to the kin-dom of God. To proclaim the cross-dead-but-risen-one as Lord reminds the principalities, powers, systems, and ideologies that currently claim the world that they have a shelf life. As Christians, we are to be a people of the *will be* and not the *as is*. We are participants in God's *to come* and not residents of the world's *right here*. Recognizing the global challenges and crises we face—including war, economic injustice, and ecological crisis—the believing skeptic is as necessary as ever.

After all, one of the believing skeptic's spiritual gifts is heresy.

THE DEACON

My parents totally think I am a heretic. Loving Jesus, the planet, justice, and the LGBTQ community at the same time is a "biblical" no-no.

Be a(n Orthodox) Heretic ;)

A Christianity with a robust account of Jesus will be heretical to the idolatrous religion that dominates so many of our hearts. To embrace this Christianity, therapeutic "believing" must die. Therapeutic belief is about the existential shape of one's faith and not (primarily) about its content. It begins by accepting the "as is" structure of our world, church, and self and then asks how we can function better as individuals and how we can make our world a bit better than we found it. In doing so, it takes for granted the very world we received and ignores the kindom's challenge to religion, culture, and politics.

My assertion is that therapeutic Christianity became possible because of modernity's secularizing trends, and it ended up as the religious ally of the very structures whose outcomes threaten life on our planet. Should the church

Being prophet and
priest is a difficult
task. Neither involves
assisting people in
ignoring the challenge of Jesus.

THE BISHOP

retain its therapeutic form of life, its professed connection to Christ will become more and more tenuous.

Prior to modernity, God was necessary and determinative in the West's account of reality. Without God, you couldn't talk about what it means to be an individual, part of a community, or a biological or economic being. In fact, all of reality was perceived as a cohesive whole with God at the top of the Great Chain of Being. During the Enlightenment, the progress of science demystified the world, taking God's necessity for the world's existence off the table. The nation-state, and eventually the democratic forms that privileged the individual's voting conscience, came to determine humanity's political arrangements, and our economic relations subsequently came to be determined by the market. Religious authority was democratized through access to the Scriptures, but it also became increasingly private—something you don't do in public or talk about at dinner.

Under these conditions, religion was no longer identified as the shared organizing structure of society; religion had to reposition itself. Though religion ceased to hold authority in reality, it did come up with all sorts of theological justifications for the minimization of its authority. These theological mythologies about the divine origin of "democratic freedom," for example, enabled the religious faithful to be faithful to other life-determining structures as though they were of God. At some point, the church decided it would rather celebrate preachers playing golf with the Pharaoh (or maybe I mean "president") than one demanding people be set free.

Rendering the story of modernity in this way highlights both the origin and shape of therapeutic Christi-

THE ELDER

I am guessing you don't like flags in the sanctuary.

anity. Therapeutic Christianity originated along with global capitalism, the nation-state, and democracy, and it has functioned so that its practitioners assumed these

THE DEACON

If by "therapeutic Christianity" you mean "my evangelical upbringing sent me into therapy," then I totally get what you mean.

three structures into their faith. These three historical and contingent structures, which mediate our social relations, determine the possibilities for life and the means by which power is exercised and distributed. Our age has committed itself to fine-tuning the fruits of humanity's social evolution. Our church ministry has committed itself to helping its members be good people, to advocating for a more benevolent system, and then to providing charity to care for society's victims.

But what if the disciples needed today are not simply good citizens, employees, and consumers? What happens when the system can't be tweaked toward justice through new regulations, the assertion of rights, and occasional redistribution of wealth?

The world doesn't have another hundred years during which the followers of Jesus put more faith in the *as is* political, economic, and ecological arrangement than Christ. Yes, there are many Christians who use their faith as a security blanket and need to be honest about their genuine doubts. Yes, too many leaders say what everyone wants to hear, performing belief on behalf of others so that serious questions are never raised. Yes, much of religion has become a marketable means to comfort and console human beings looking to ignore suffering, responsibility, and the absence of meaning. But underneath the hidden doubts are some strong and unquestioned beliefs about the finality of our human and ecological relations.

Perhaps the most problematic belief in Christianity isn't the inerrancy of Scripture, strict Calvinism, religious exclusivism, or "open but not affirming." Perhaps life on our planet is most threatened by our unconscious faith to the *as is* assumptions integral to therapeutic Christianity. Christianity must be freed from its role atop the symbolic chain of being and take another form that doesn't assume the *as is* structures of our suicidal machine are final. This is the very pattern of engagement Jesus has with his own historical situation and one to which we are being called by crucified people today.

For Christians, the kin-dom of God made present in the ministry of Jesus is the permanent coming horizon of each and every moment through the resurrection. The resurrection of the cross-dead Jesus is God's confrontation of each and every inherited structure and assumption about the world as it is with the prophetic critique and eschatological hope of the new creation's *will be*. The resurrection, both then and now, proclaims the contingency of every present order.

THE ACOLYTE

Isn't it interesting that being theologically conservative can make you politically radical?

The shape of a faith formed in God's promise of what *will be* is definitely not therapeutic. While recognizing the progress made through democracies, nation-states, and capitalism, a Christian cannot assume this is the best we can do. We can't make faith a means of cultivating a kinder, gentler, and slightly improved version of the world we are handed. If we are honest about our global situation, we know we can't. We must insist that humanity dream and create a more just and equitable way of relating to each other and to our planet. We can do better.

We need more Christian heretics. We need Christians whose previously assumed and unquestioned allegiance to global capitalism is shaken. We need heretical Christian communities who reject a utilitarian and mechanistic relationship to creation. Heretical Christians and prophetic Christianity are actually interesting in a world where much of Christianity isn't so interesting anymore. A Christianity given shape by what will be can never be content with what already is, and that is exciting.

It is inspiring.

That's when I say, "Thank God for that most awesome homeless Jew."

Acknowledgments

This book and the entire series come from some amazing friendships. There are the three people who helped found the second Fuller Theological Seminary in our dining room: my parents and most awesome brother Steven Fuller. Frank Tupper and Philip Clayton are both theological mentors and friends who have prodded and poked my brain. Bo and Chad have been my audiological brothers, who have rocked the mic on the podcast with me since 2008 and rehearsed many of these ideas before our listeners' ears. I imagine there will be some solid cryptomnesia in the text. Peter Rollins, who survived living with the entire Fuller family while I wrote this book, assures me that if he had to believe in a God with a magic kid it would be the version I describe. I am pretty sure that was quality Irish encouragement, and I really appreciated it.

I also want to thank Tony, Joe, and the rest of the Fortress team. It's a real privilege to work with such awesome people. Beyond his work at Fortress, Tony Jones has been a friend of mine for over ten years now. With his encouragement, support, and wisdom, he is getting real close to ruining his reputation as a hard ass. Luckily, he managed to fit enough "constructive criticism" into the notes on the book. Tim Burnette was the master of editing, clarifying, distilling, and de-dyslexifying each chapter in the book. I also want to thank Diane, Bill, Grace, Helene, Adam, Eric, Jeff, Rolf, and Donna, who all have books coming out in the series. I can't believe I get to partner with such stellar scholars and communicators over the next couple years.

To all the Homebrewed Christianity Podcast listeners and supporters, I want to say thank you. I love creating the podcast and remain honored so many of you not only listen but join in the conversation.

For over fifteen years I have been a student minister to some of the coolest adults in the making. I had the honor of facilitating 118 students' journeys through confirmation, and so much of this is shaped by the questions, insights, and stories of those students.

Lastly, I want to thank my family. Being Elgin and Khora's dad brings me indescribable joy. That joy is intensified because I get to share it with my best friend and partner, Alecia. Alecia and I met freshman year of college, which means she has known and loved every obnoxious version of me I mention in the book and more. Her friendship has been the greatest gift of my life.

Tripp

Notes

Chapter 1

1. Pliny, *Letters* 10.96–97. You can read the entire exchange here: www.earlychristianwritings.com/text/pliny.html.

2. Søren Kierkegaard, *Concluding Unscientific Postscript to the Philosophical Fragments*, trans. Howard Hong and Edna Hong (Princeton: Princeton University Press, 1992), 204.

3. Yes, I do have really vivid dreams where I argue with dead philosophers and theologians. Not only that, but Jesus tends to show up in the form of Bob Marley.

4. Roger Haight has a similar outline in his magisterial Christology, *Jesus the Symbol of God* (Maryknoll, NY: Orbis, 1999), 330–34.

5. 1 Pet. 3:15.

6. "Doxology" means a worshipful praise to God.

7. About that last rule, it's really cool. Just think about it. If you are praying for your enemies and learning to forgive without counting, then when it comes to understanding divine judgment you are much less likely to think God created all seven billion people on this planet in God's own image and then is going to end up putting five billion of them in hell.

8. This is discussed in chapter 6.

Chapter 2

1. "Son of Man" was a mysterious figure in Jewish Apocalyptic literature that was to come at the end of the age. Check out Dan. 7:13-14 and 1 Enoch 37–71 to see this righteous heavenly judge in action.

2. Mark 12:18.

3. If I got to put together a Jesus film, I would have this zealot uprising be where Joseph, Jesus' human papa, died. Scholars have argued recently that Jesus and his family likely worked in the construction of Sepphoris, a capital city and symbol of Roman oppression. If Jesus was in Galilee at the time of the uprising, he would have been familiar with or even seen the aftermath. If his dad was among the crucified . . .

4. Flavius Josephus, *The Jewish War* 2.169–74.

5. Monkish is also the name of the best brewery in LA. Its founder and head brewer Henry is a master at brewing delicious Belgian beer like the monks. He also has a PhD in feminist criticism of the New Testament and lets us host live podcast events at the brewery. So if you see "monkish" on a bottle, don't pass on it.

6. Mark 10:37.

7. 2 Cor. 5:16.

Chapter 3

1. Mark 1:18.

2. Matt. 6:9.

3. Robert Hamerton-Kelly describes in systematic and persuasive fashion how "far from being a sexist symbol, the 'father' was for Jesus a weapon chosen to combat what we call 'sexism.'" *God the Father: Theology and Patriarchy in the Teaching of Jesus* (Philadelphia: Fortress Press, 1979), 103.

4. Matt. 18:22.

5. Matt. 5:28, 44.

6. John 20:21.

Chapter 4

1. Pheme Perkins, "The Synoptic Gospels and the Acts of the Apostles: Telling the Christian Story," in *The Cambridge Companion to Biblical Interpretation*, ed. John Barton (Cambridge: Cambridge University Press, 1998), 241–58.

2. Mark 1:3.

3. Mark 1:11.

4. See 2 Sam. 7:14 and Isa. 42:1-4.

5. Many New Testament scholars believe that in Rom. 1:3-4 Paul is quoting a popular tradition in the church. This would mean that prior to Paul, Jesus was already "declared to be Son of God

with power according to the spirit of holiness by resurrection from the dead."

6. Mark 1:1, 15:39.

7. Chapter 6 will discuss just what a "low" Christology means in depth.

8. Luke 1:52-53.

9. Luke 23:46.

10. Luke 4:18-19.

11. Isa. 61:2.

12. John 8:42.

13. John 18:6.

14. Matt. 15:22-28.

Chapter 5

1. That Geneva line was sarcastic. Calvin helped establish the town, and they even exiled him! Of course, that was tame compared to Michael Servetus, who was burned at the stake for having a non-Trinitarian Christology. Whether Calvin ordered that execution is a matter of historical debate.

2. Phil. 2:8.

3. OK, Luther did not mandate this particular form of property reallocation, but a friend of mine who happens to be a Luther scholar said it happened at least three times, and we know that Luther was intimately connected with two of them. Therefore, I decided to call it a trend that I would talk, write, and tell people about, in hopes that a person of means would like to bring this model back. Should they have an interest, they can contact me at tripp@homebrewedchristianity.com.

4. "Cooties," *Urban Dictionary*, user-submitted definitions, http://www.urbandictionary.com/define.php?term=Cooties.

Chapter 6

1. Rom. 1:20.

2. Of course, this experience does not require you to believe in God at all. You could instead be struck by the sheer luck required for a thinking, talking, and farting piece of stardust to have the opportunity to look at distant relatives twinkling in the night sky. This important question will be discussed in the HBC *Guide to God*.

3. Col. 1:15.

4. 1 Cor. 2:7, Col. 1:15, and John 1:1-18.

5. Justin Martyr (I.40).

6. Stephen T. Davis, ed., *Encountering Jesus: A Debate on Christology* (Atlanta: John Knox Press, 1988).

7. John 1:1-5.

Chapter 7

1. Jonathan Steele, "Forgotten Victims" *Guardian*, May 20, 2002, http://www.theguardian.com/world/2002/may/20/afghanistan.comment.

2. Mark 15:34.

3. Jürgen Moltmann, *The Crucified God: The Cross of Christ as the Foundation and Criticism of Christian Theology* (Minneapolis: Fortress Press, 1993), 246.

4. Albert L. Winseman, "Women in the Clergy: Perception and Reality," *Gallup*, Religion and Social Trends, March 30, 2004, http://www.gallup.com/poll/11146/women-clergy-perception-reality.aspx.

5. Prov. 8:22-31.

6. Wisd. of Sol. 7:26-28.

7. Matt. 11:19.

8. 1 Cor. 1:24 and John 10:10.

9. Prov. 8:35.

10. Elizabeth A. Johnson, *She Who Is: The Mystery of God in Feminist Theological Discourse* (New York: Crossroad, 1992), 161.

11. Ibid.

Chapter 8

1. Mark 8:29.

2. Philip Clayton and I explored this in more detail in *Transforming Christian Theology: For Church and Society* (Minneapolis: Fortress Press, 2010).

3. Isa. 4:2.

4. Jürgen Moltmann, *Ethics of Hope* (Minneapolis: Fortress Press, 2012), 300.

5. Elizabeth A. Johnson, *Ask the Beasts: Darwin and the God of Love* (London: Continuum, 2014).